DARK
SISTER

Books by Lynn V. Andrews

Medicine Woman

Spirit Woman

Jaguar Woman

The Woman of Wyrrd

Love and Power

Tree of Dreams

The Power Deck

Teachings Around the Sacred Wheel

Writing Spirit

DARK
SISTER

A Sorcerer's Love Story

Lynn V. Andrews

Illustrations by Ginny Joyner

JEREMY P. TARCHER/PENGUIN

a member of Penguin Group (USA) Inc.

New York

JEREMY P. TARCHER/PENGUIN
Published by the Penguin Group
Penguin Group (USA) Inc., 375 Hudson Street, New York, New York 10014, USA •
Penguin Group (Canada), 90 Eglinton Avenue East, Suite 700, Toronto, Ontario M4P 2Y3,
Canada (a division of Pearson Penguin Canada Inc.) • Penguin Books Ltd, 80 Strand,
London WC2R 0RL, England • Penguin Ireland, 25 St Stephen's Green, Dublin 2, Ireland
(a division of Penguin Books Ltd) • Penguin Group (Australia), 250 Camberwell Road,
Camberwell, Victoria 3124, Australia (a division of Pearson Australia Group Pty Ltd) •
Penguin Books India Pvt Ltd, 11 Community Centre, Panchsheel Park, New Delhi–110 017,
India • Penguin Group (NZ), 67 Apollo Drive, Rosedale, North Shore 0745, Auckland,
New Zealand (a division of Pearson New Zealand Ltd) • Penguin Books (South Africa)
(Pty) Ltd, 24 Sturdee Avenue, Rosebank, Johannesburg 2196, South Africa

Penguin Books Ltd, Registered Offices: 80 Strand, London WC2R 0RL, England

First Jeremy P. Tarcher/Penguin edition 2007
Copyright © 1995, 2007 by Lynn V. Andrews
Dark Sister was originally published by HarperCollins in 1995.

Most Tarcher/Penguin books are available at special quantity discounts for bulk purchase
for sales promotions, premiums, fund-raising, and educational needs. Special books or book
excerpts also can be created to fit specific needs. For details, write Penguin Group (USA) Inc.
Special Markets, 375 Hudson Street, New York, NY 10014.

Library of Congress Cataloging-in-Publication Data
Andrews, Lynn V.
Dark sister : a sorcerer's love story / Lynn V. Andrews ; illustrations by Ginny Joyner.
p.   cm.—(Women's studies)
Originally published: HarperCollins Publishers, c1995.
ISBN-13: 978-1-58542-579-2
1. Shamanism—Miscellanea.   2. Women—Religious life.   I. Joyner, Ginny.   II. Title.
BP610.A54134   2007   2007017421
299'.93—dc22

Printed in the United States of America
1   3   5   7   9   10   8   6   4   2

Book design by Caitlin Daniels

While the author has made every effort to provide accurate telephone numbers and Internet
addresses at the time of publication, neither the publisher nor the author assumes any responsibility for errors, or for changes that occur after publication. Further, the publisher
does not have any control over and does not assume any responsibility for author or third-
party websites or their content.

For Jaguar Woman and all those dedicated to the art of illumination

Many of the names and locations have been changed to protect the privacy of those involved.

Our deepest fear is not that we are inadequate. Our deepest fear is that we are powerful beyond measure. It is our light, not our darkness, that most frightens us. We ask ourselves, who am I to be brilliant, gorgeous, talented, and fabulous? Actually, who are you not to be? You are a child of God. Your playing small doesn't serve the world. There is nothing enlightened about shrinking so that other people will not feel insecure around you. We were born to make manifest the glory of God that is within us. It is not in just some of us; it is in everyone. And as we let our own light shine, we unconsciously give people permission to do the same. As we are liberated from our own fear, our presence automatically liberates others.

—Marianne Williamson, from *A Return to Love*, as quoted by Nelson Mandela in his inaugural speech as President of South Africa, May 1994

contents

Introduction

"May I ask a question?" the woman at the microphone said. "I would like to ask you what you feel about the negative impact of the feminist movement. It seems that more than ever one woman turns against another woman in her efforts to get success."

The question pulled me back into the auditorium. I was standing on a stage in front of 250 people at a gathering in Seattle, Washington. The rain was sheeting down outside, and my mind had momentarily flashed to memories of my childhood, growing up in the Northwest, seemingly always cloudy and damp.

"Do you mean," I asked, "women in the same field? Are you talking about women in professional life? Could you clarify that question, please?"

"I'm asking about women in general, women who are in professional life, but also those in every walk of life. I seem to find in my own life a tremendous amount of difficulty. When I became successful in a Fortune 500 company in Seattle, it seemed that other women—women who had been my friends—betrayed me, tried to pull me down, and certainly did not stand by me in my success."

I could see that the woman was very upset by this subject. Her hands shook slightly as she held the microphone, and I could see that she was trying to fight back tears.

I had a glimpse in my mind of a ceremonial circle, powerful women of the Sisterhood of the Shields in the Yucatán jungle. I felt the smoke from the central fire in my blood.

"I understand your pain," I said, the vision fading, "because

I certainly have experienced it myself. All I can say to you is that I think we are in an adolescent era, coming to the end of it, where we are tearing down everything that we have known to be traditionally solid. We are tearing down our heroes, our heroines. We are leaving, however, little to replace what we have destroyed.

"I find that women in a patriarchal system seem to adapt themselves to that system by becoming like the men that they decry. There is, in essence, a death dance in action at this moment. Most ancient cultures and prophets have spoken of our time in history. Many ancient calendars, the Mayan calendar, many East Indian and Native American calendars, so many prophecies around the world, talk about the end of a certain era coming up very shortly. As this energy begins to shift, surely the controlling energy and power does not want to lose its hold, and someone might ask me, 'Who are you talking about?' I don't know if it's a who or a they or a them. I think there is a collective energy form that is trying to stay as it always has been, the status quo of predominantly patriarchal energy.

"What is happening, I believe, is that women have made enormous strides in public life and economically. And now we're moving into a time of much deeper spirituality. Much of that spirituality revolves around exploring the Goddess, Native American traditions, shamanic trainings, all kinds of spirituality that relate to Mother Earth and the firstness of woman. This is a time of tremendous flux and change. As a result, men in power are not only creating a force field that would pull us down at every moment, it seems, but women also seem, for some reason, to be caught up in this vortex, and without thinking, I believe, end up creating tremendous difficulty for their sisters."

My thoughts raced ahead to Manitoba. After the lecture, I was leaving for the airport to fly to Canada and be with my teachers. I had had a tension in my solar plexus for days, a sense that something mysterious was about to happen.

"But why would we not support each other?" asked the woman, standing tall and seemingly emotionally stricken in the center of the room. "Why would women not support one another? I support my friends when they become successful. I support my sisters."

"Yes," I answered, "and that is very wonderful, and so do I. That doesn't mean that all people do what we expect them to do, as you well know. So it is an interesting process that we need to examine from our hearts and from our wisdom of what we know it is like to be a woman in the world. We have been under siege for so long. When you think that nine million women and children were burned during the Inquisition, you realize that we have a long, even cellular, history and remembrance of that kind of pain and subjugation to ignorance.

"Many women have said to me, when they see one woman turning against another, that we have so much anger toward the world for not being heard and not being recognized and not being able to be who we truly are in life, that it doesn't matter whom we hurt, we just want to lash out. Maybe that's true, or maybe it's not, but I think the course of darkness, which some people may call evil, perhaps chooses no sex. And even if it's woman against woman or man against man, the issue is not woman or man. The issue to be examined is, in fact, the darkness itself."

DARK
SISTER

Prologue
Seduction

The dust rose like steam from the tires of Jake Martin's old green pickup truck as he drove a dirt frontage road from Patagonia toward Nogales in southern Arizona. It was an early hot summer evening, and the clouds, like sheep, dotted the horizon. Jake was on his way to his cousin's wedding in Mexico. He had left the reservation, where he was a patrolman, about two hours before. All day he had felt a little queasy—probably getting that cold. How could he have known that he was being stalked?

Long ago, when he was a boy in Canada, he and his family had lived on a reservation in Manitoba, but his mother had decided to visit a long-lost sister on the reservation in Arizona. After they had arrived, Jake met the reservation cop and had idolized him his whole life. All he wanted to do was be the reservation cop, and so he had become one. Jake was in his late thirties. He had not married, but he expected in his forties he would settle down and would surely raise a family. As he bumped down the road toward Mexico, he thought of his old spirit guide, Geronimo, and how he hated going into Mexico, much as Geronimo had. Looking around at the mountains surrounding him, he thought of the San Pedro River Valley on the other side of Tombstone, Cochise's stronghold, and Geronimo, the great Apache warrior. He felt the power of that man in his breast and thought about what it must have been like a hundred years ago in this beautiful valley.

Striations of an orange and pink sunset streaked the sky. As he looked ahead through the dirty dust-laden windshield of his truck, he saw a lone figure in the distance, standing by the side of the road. He blinked several times, thinking that he was imagining things. This was a lonely and deserted road. That's why he had chosen it instead of the two-lane highway that stretched from Benson down into Mexico.

He slowed his truck as he approached a stand of trees off to the right and rolled down his window, dust and dirt wedging into the door and puffing onto his lap. The figure that he had seen was gone, and he decided to park the truck by the side of the road and relieve himself behind one of the trees. As he stood behind a thicket of bushes he looked into the dusky darkness and noticed for the first time a small stone Mayan-like ruin that had steps up toward the sky and the tops of the trees, like the temples for blood sacrifice that he had seen in Mexico farther south. It was some kind of ruin or temple that he had never seen before, though he had been on this road a hundred times.

Still staring at the magnificent stone edifice before him, he walked out of the shadows and into the pink evening light. Then he saw the figure of a woman standing near the entrance of the temple. He was amazed and fascinated. He walked toward the temple door, and as he did so, the woman approached him.

She was easily the most beautiful woman he had ever seen, with long black hair that reached to her waist and swung gently from side to side. She wore sandals and a skirt of an unusual weave. Sewn into the fabric were little mirrors, reflecting the sunset. She wore a white blouse of thin cotton material, and he could see her breasts moving voluptuously as she walked toward him. What tempted him the most was this feeling of warmth, like the first blush of fine whiskey, that was enveloping his being like a dense fog. A passion overcame him unlike anything he had experienced before. He couldn't imagine what was happening to him, but it was so pleasurable that he didn't question it for more than a moment.

Sin Corazón reached out her hand to Jake. Gently she placed her hand on his arm so that she could contact his energy field and make it part of her own. She took a deep breath as she began her dance of hypnotism and seduction. She could see in Jake's eyes that he was surprised by the effect of her touch. She could see the confusion and then his decision simply not to question what was happening.

"Will you help me?" she asked, her voice so soft and lovely.

"What has happened?" he stammered, looking around.

"Oh, it's my car. I had a flat tire up the road."

"What are you doing here?" It was the middle of nowhere.

He thought for a moment of not having seen a car. Well, then, it must be down farther south.

"If you'll just get in my truck, I'll drive you to it. I don't have much time," he said. "I'm going to a wedding."

"How fortuitous," she said.

"What do you mean?" he asked, bewildered by her beauty.

"That you're on your way to a wedding," she said with a toss of her head, her raven black hair brushing across her fingers.

He stared at the temple in the shadows behind her. The last vestiges of the sunset glinted off the higher corbels at the top.

"I've never seen this ruin before. Do you happen to know what it is?" he asked her. "Or who built it?"

"Why, yes, I happen to know a great deal about this temple," she said, lowering her eyes mysteriously. "Come." Taking his hand in a very sensuous manner, she led him. "The temple is built by the shadowy dreams of magic and mystery. Come! Let me show you."

"Oh, yes," he said.

She turned and stopped for a moment. "Would you care to come into the temple with me?" she asked.

"Yes, of course. I would love to see it. It's very beautiful, but how . . ." His voice trailed off as she led him through the temple door, massive stone pillars on either side. Jake could not take his eyes off her. He would have followed her into fire.

They walked onto the stone floor and through the entryway into a small vaulted room that was obviously meant for some kind of ancient ceremony or ritual. In the center was a raised stone slab. The woman took a blood red blanket that was rolled up by the side of it and placed it on the waist-high slab of stone. She turned to Jake, who was rigid with passion for this woman. He barely looked around. His eyes were only for Sin Corazón, and nothing else mattered.

She began to unbutton his shirt. Within moments they were lying on the red blanket, passionately embraced. Once he heard an owl, which for him was a harbinger of death and extreme change in his life, and he should have listened. He should have gotten up from the stone and run for his very life. The odd feeling at the edge of his consciousness was not strong enough to combat his passion, or hers.

As he made his last thrust into her body, he looked into the dark eyes of Sin Corazón. He screamed in terror as he saw the face not of the dusky beauty of moments ago, but the face of an ancient old woman with wrinkles and lines beyond description.

Sin Corazón enjoyed shape shifting and making her victims see a vision of horror. Her black silky hair had turned to wild gray masses of mats and tangles. She sat with her legs around him and raised her arms and her face toward the heavens, and she laughed with the cackling laughter of a sorceress who had had her way with her victim.

A sickening feeling was coming over Jake. A gash of orange light fell brutally over their bodies from an opening in the tower above. Again he screamed in fright and recoiled, falling off the slab onto the floor, trying to gather his clothes and his senses. Sin Corazón continued to laugh. She said nothing. She had her revenge once again toward all men, who always wore the face of her ex-husband, and she had replenished her power by taking the power of this virile man. As he glanced one last time toward her, the hatred in her flashing eyes was awesome.

He could not walk. "Why?" he asked. He felt as if the life force had been drained from him. For a long time he sat on the floor with his head in his hands, trying to regain his balance.

As his last vestiges of power drained out of him like blood into the sand, he fell over and lay on the stone floor, unconscious. He did not hear Sin Corazón drive away in his truck. His dreams were nightmares of jackals tearing him to pieces and coyotes running away with his soul.

When he finally awakened, it was early morning. The wedding was over. He had missed everything. He struggled to get up, but he could not. As he looked around, at first he did not know where he was. There was no temple, no magnificent stone facade, only a clearing in the trees.

As he lay in the dust, he looked to where his truck had been, and it was gone. It would be many years before Jake would regain any sense of health or strength. He became a legend in his time, a man who walked the streets with only half a mind, muttering about a beautiful young woman who had seduced him and then turned into an old hag. His spirit guides and medicine had left him, and he was alone.

1
Darkness Defines the Light

Agnes perched like an old buzzard on the railing of her porch. The crisp northern air was laden with the scent of pine and wildflowers. Rocking back and forth in a rickety bentwood rocker, I watched Crow peck bread crumbs off the ground. He scolded me, cawing, and turned his head, watching me with his yellow eye. I had arrived at her cabin in Manitoba the day before, and I was grateful just to sit.

Agnes, wearing a jean skirt and a bright red blouse with her gray hair in thick braids, held up a tiny crystal to a ray of sunlight streaming through branches of a poplar tree. Suddenly, a burning flash of prismatic light, laserlike and profoundly bright, ricocheted off the crystal and into my eye. My head thumped back against the rocker as I yelled, "Good grief, Agnes, that hurt!"

"Sometimes the light can be too bright, too painful to look at."

"No kidding," I said, rubbing my eye.

Agnes, her Native American face creased and weathered from the years, settled her hands in her lap and looked off in the distance. "So," she continued, "if you can't yet adjust to the light of something, you perceive it in another way."

"What are you getting at?" I asked.

Agnes rubbed her belly. "You open your body-mind and perceive light like Ruby does. She absorbs light and shadow through her intent and has learned to see that way with her blind eyes. That's why no one is more aware than Ruby. There is nothing that she cannot see—even in total darkness. For her, there is always light, and it can no longer be taken from her."

"That's nice, Agnes," I said, "but you could have warned me."

"Sometimes a truth has to hurt a bit to be remembered." Agnes swirled the leaves in her mug of tea, poured out the liquid, and dumped the wet leaves into the palm of her hand. "Close your eyes," she ordered, "and lean back." Gently, Agnes placed a poultice of herbal tea leaves over my eyelid. "Does that help?" she asked, poking me in the ribs.

"Yes, yes," I said gratefully, relaxing as the heat penetrated and soothed my eye. "Thank you."

Several minutes passed as I sat in my self-imposed darkness.

"Can you see what I'm doing?" Agnes asked. I heard her feet shuffling on the worn floorboards of the porch.

"Of course not, Agnes," I said.

"Can you tell what I'm doing now; can you see me now?"

"I can tell that you're moving around, Agnes, but all I can see is darkness."

Agnes paused in silence for a moment. Then I heard her voice farther away and above, as if she were perched on the roof.

"When you see only darkness, you can perceive almost nothing that is happening around you—it's as if you are blind, even with your eyes open."

"Okay," I said, still not getting it.

"It's very simple," Agnes said. "The light, sunlight or wisdom, illuminates what is there. Simple and true—ignorance is born from not seeing what is there in front of you. When you live in the darkness of your soul, you cannot see the truth, a chair, an idea, or whatever is in existence for your benefit."

I sat for a long time, following Agnes's idea like a thread in a weaving. Finally, I swept the tea leaves into my hand and opened my eyes.

I was stunned to see that the moon was up and darkness had descended on the cabin. I heard a crow in the distance. Agnes was nowhere to be seen. I had an odd tugging sensation in my stomach, as if something very important was about to happen.

2
The Storyteller

The next morning Agnes announced to us, with a g.
expression on her face, that we must leave immediately i
southern Mexico.

Since the night before, the sense of foreboding in my stomach had not left. I knew that Agnes would explain this decision when it was time. In all my years of apprenticeship to her,
I had learned never to question a decision of this kind. The
women in the Sisterhood of the Shields are always on the
move, and always for important reasons.

"Even as tired as I am, I look forward to seeing Zoila and
Jaguar Woman again," I said. Ruby and Agnes stopped gathering their things for the journey and sat down on either side of
me at the table.

In her customary manner, Agnes ran the palms of her hands
over the old wooden boards of the table, feeling the knotholes,
the nicks, and the grain of the wood.

"You know, you've written many books, my daughter. And
they are good books, books with consciousness that teach people things about our ways. But it is time that you learned something new about your art. It is time you became a storyteller."

"What do you mean?" I asked.

Ruby wore turquoise beads over a yellow blouse and jeans.
Her blind eyes were blue like the sky in her darkly tanned
face. From the other side of the table, she cleared her throat, as
if to get my attention, and smoothed her sleek salt-and-pepper
hair. It was braided, tied back with woven yellow yarn, and
was hanging down her back. With both hands she twisted her
hair up onto her head.

...t you learn the art of the true Twisted Hair, the "It is/ler."

sacred...ght that was something that I understood."

"B/u understand it from one dimension, but now it is "...t to learn another dimension."

im/h't understand," I said.

...ell, you will soon enough," Ruby said. "You have never ...ten in what you call third person."

"This is true," I answered.

"It is time that you see the art of the Twisted Hair in a different way. As you know, there is great power and sacredness in words, enough power to strengthen your abilities and your will."

Agnes, on the other side, again began to speak. "As you perhaps remember, Jaguar Woman is one of the greatest Twisted Hairs among us. She is a consummate Storyteller."

"What makes her such a great Storyteller?" I asked.

"Because she knows how to take herself out of the story," Ruby answered for Agnes. "She knows how to completely remove herself, as if she were a fly on the wall with no self-importance. If she happens to be in the story, she speaks of herself as if she is simply part of the tale. She weaves a sacred dream. She takes words like threads, magnificently luminous and colored with the light of creation, and weaves them together with magic and power into a tapestry so that the story lives for you. She is like no other Storyteller I have been graced to hear."

"And is that not an oral tradition?" I asked.

"Yes, it is, but now it is going to be your task to listen to a Storyteller and to record in book form what you have seen and heard. There is much ahead for you in the next few weeks. There are great events ahead of you, Little Wolf, and if you do not take the right path at the crossroads of power, you are going to find yourself in the greatest danger of your life. I want you to tune yourself and bring yourself into the center of your own truth, because you're going to need all the resources that you have at your command to survive."

I took a deep breath and looked at my two teachers, checking for a glint of humor. Were they kidding me or trying to elicit some kind of reaction?

Agnes reached out her hand, strong and tough from years of work, and touched my arm.

"Lynn, we are speaking with the utmost truth, across my sacred pipe. We are going to the southern parts of Mexico. We are going because of something that I do not want to explain. I simply want you to experience it. During our journey in the South, it is my hope that Jaguar Woman will relate to us with her extraordinary abilities the story that has unfolded into her life and now becomes part of our own.

"There is much for you to learn in these stories. Be aware. Do not miss anything. Your impeccability is needed at this time for you to survive with your spirit intact. Do you hear me like you hear the wind?" she asked.

I looked into her eyes for a long time. I felt every pore on my body perspire and a kind of fear that I had not felt. Never before had my teachers approached me in such a manner. Then I put myself into the center of my power, and I realized that I was stronger than I had ever been. It was appropriate to be tested by them at this time.

"My teachers—Agnes, Ruby—I hear you. I understand that there are tests, that there are moments of great importance ahead of me. I will stand in my power to the best of my ability. I thank you for telling me. I will listen to Jaguar Woman's words, and I will write of her stories to the best of my ability. I face this journey with great excitement and joy. Thank you for including me on this path of heart."

They each gave me a gift. Agnes extended her hand and gave me her herkemer crystal that, small as it was, caught the light with prismatic colors, throwing the spectrum around the cabin walls. Ruby reached out her hand and gave me a tiny cowrie.

"This shell was sewn into the wedding dress of my mother many long, long years ago. I wish for you to have it. Put both of these magical gifts into your medicine bag and wear it around your neck until we return. These are given with our love and our trust in your intent."

In the hour before we left, I went out to do ceremony.

3

A Conjurer's Dream

I sat next to a flowing stream near the cabin on my talking stone, the stone I always used when I was calling in my spirit helpers and searching for a healing. I looked up through the treetops. The sun was in the proper position in the sky for my dreaming. Taking off my medicine bag, which hung around my neck, I emptied the cowrie shells and crystals into the palm of my hand, and held them, closing my eyes, dreaming with my spirit helpers about the journey ahead.

I listened to the flowing water and the high wind singing through the trees. And then, in my dreaming, I saw a beautiful woman whom I recognized, but not clearly enough to name. She was solitary and despondent from a sickness of the spirit that no one seemed to understand.

Again, I felt an uneasiness in the pit of my stomach. I moved the shells and crystals from one hand to the other, letting the play of light reflect on them. It was through touch and the light that my divining came. I watched the sunlight play on the river water as it tumbled by, almost noiselessly now, because there had not been much rain. I tried to take my mind away from this sense of uneasiness, but as I moved deeper and deeper into my healing trance, I sensed something strange in my sacred vision, something that I had never seen before. Into my mind's eye came a brilliant ruby light, the color of passion and anger, the color of blood in the sunset. All at once I heard a cracking sound like a branch being torn from a tree and snapped in two. Startled by the violent sound, I clutched the shells and crystals until they cut into the heel of my palm.

Slowly, in my mind's eye, I experienced the tumultuousness

of a storm as strong winds whipped into a funnel of light and darkness around me. Out of that spiraling movement came the masklike face of a beautiful woman with long black hair and the death eyes of an evil sorceress, intent on only harm and revenge.

Could she be Sin Corazón? She looked so different, so violent. Fear crawled up my spine. Then, centering myself, I traced the energy lines from this woman's heart and found the pain and the sadness of a woman who had explored the talents of a black magician somewhere deep in the southern jungles and had become his victim. I saw the face of tragedy and theft, but I knew not how this painful vision related to me. Again, I shook the shells and the crystals in my hand and placed them out in front of me, at random with my other crystals, looking at the formation as if I were looking at tea leaves in the bottom of a cup. I saw the family relatedness, somehow, and that she was a powerful elder. She looked like Jaguar Woman, standing between the black-haired sorceress and an old man who was also very powerful.

That drew me back into the pain in my stomach. The uneasiness had turned into a shooting pain. I saw that I needed to tell Agnes and Ruby that, indeed, there was going to be an attempted theft. For a moment I saw a fabulous star ruby, more beautiful than any precious stone I had ever seen. I recognized it as the Shaman's Jewel, the most sacred object of the Sisterhood of the Shields. I knew that its value was not in money but in its sacredness and its ability to hold and transmit the healing power of light. Then I saw a circle of powerful native women protecting it: the Sisterhood.

I took a deep breath. The visions subsided. I gathered my things and went back to the cabin.

I told Agnes and Ruby what I had seen. "Was it Sin Corazón? What has happened to her? She looks terrifying and evil!"

"Come. We must go," Agnes said. "You will see soon enough."

4

Banishment

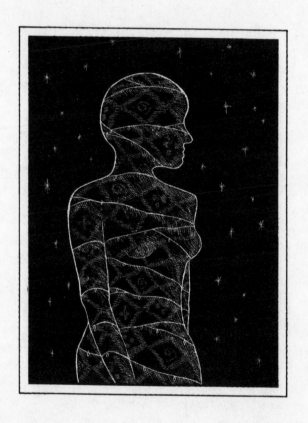

Dark clouds crowded the horizon. An unusually cool wind had come up from the west, bringing the smell of salt from the sea to a circle of women of power in the mountains of southern Mexico.

This was the Sisterhood of the Shields, forty-four in number, who had memorized and handed down from sister to daughter to apprentice throughout time the ancient wisdom and power of woman. For all the history of the Sisterhood, never had one of them fallen away. This ceremony, happening for the first time, was our urgent reason for traveling south.

In the center of this special group of women, each one more powerful, more full of vitality and creative energy than the next, stood Jaguar Woman. She wore her carved ceremonial jaguar mask, which she had worn throughout her ritualistic involvement with the Sisterhood. We were solemn this day and full of sadness for the purpose of our meeting. Many of us had traveled a great distance. Standing next to Jaguar Woman was her apprentice, Sin Corazón, whose name when translated into English means "No Heart." A great deal of painful energy was passing between them. Jaguar Woman took a black strip of cotton material that had been woven with smbols and colored threads. Various elements hanging on this cotton material represented darkness, separation, finality, and broken relationships. Jaguar Woman wrapped this around the waist and the shoulders of Sin Corazón.

The ceremony was devastating in its proportion of sadness and pain. We all added our energy to this ceremony. Yet Sin Corazón, instead of crying, instead of feeling sorrow or any kind of remorse, was very angry. Her face echoed a coldness and a steely resilience not unlike the power I felt in Jaguar Woman. There was a kind of hatred, an almost black gaze to the eyes of death within her face.

This is a woman, I thought to myself, whom I had loved very much and thought I had known. Now it was obvious that there were many aspects of her I had not known at all. The dark passion of her grief for her lost husband, understandably very hurtful and deep, was still beyond my comprehension. In the jungles not far from where we held our ceremonies, she had slipped away into the worlds of dark sorcery and mystery with a teacher unknown to me.

The pathways that Sin Corazón had chosen were unfamiliar. Not that I felt above the darkness that she had involved herself in, because I think there are times in life when all of us are capable of doing unbelievable things. If we had to protect a threatened child, not one of us within this circle would not be capable of murder. But this was not an issue of self-defense; this was a question of cold-blooded power plays in the world.

I remembered Sin Corazón coming into a gathering we had held a few years before. I remembered her flamboyance, her intelligence, her ability to seize the situation and take hold of it in a way that wasn't pleasurable to any of the rest of us. I remember how she disrupted the circle with her friction and her ability to turn one woman against another. She had obviously spent a long time stalking the two women who became involved in the argument that destroyed the purpose, quality, and integrity of what we were trying to accomplish.

That was one of the talents that Sin Corazón used in the world. She always came in looking as if what she was doing was good and kind and important. Instead, disruption reigned. Nothing was accomplished: only darkness and confusion and broken trust descended upon the people around her.

Jaguar Woman pulled on the black material wrapped around her apprentice. She was almost dragging her against her will. Sin Corazón was certainly not foolish enough not to follow a teacher of such extraordinary power as Jaguar Woman, but in the way that she walked I could see that Sin Corazón now considered herself Jaguar Woman's equal. In the way Jaguar Woman was handling her apprentice, it was evident that she knew it was an aspect of fate to have lost her apprentice. Jaguar Woman's attitude was a kind of deference, almost the approach of a tired mother to an errant child who does not know what it is doing. It was as if Jaguar Woman could see Sin Corazón heading for a wall at eighty miles per hour and knew that the teacher cannot remove that wall. If the apprentice must hit that wall, then so be it.

Finally, Jaguar Woman stopped, faced her apprentice, and wrapped the black material around Sin Corazón's head, covering her eyes. Then, quickly, she wrapped the rest of her body like a mummy so that Sin Corazón could not move. Then, from around her own waist, Jaguar Woman unwrapped a very long and ancient sash that had been embroidered over and over again to symbolize the sacred ceremonies that she had performed with her apprentices over time. Wrapping one end of the sash around Sin Corazón's waist, she wrapped the other end around her own. Then, taking her sharp obsidian blade used only for ceremony, she stood with her arms up to the sky, cried to the universe, and then chanted in Quiché.

Then, with one powerful motion, Jaguar Woman cut the sash in half. Its symbolism was no longer intact; it's significance was over and finished. The sash fell to the ground. As if it were an obstacle, Jaguar Woman stepped over it. Then turning her apprentice to the left—to the direction of darker powers, instead of to the right, sunwise—she unwrapped the black material until Sin Corazón stood in the center of our silent circle.

I could not believe what I had witnessed. I had never heard of any such thing, any kind of banishment, any kind of falling away, ever, among these women. What had just occurred here would take me a long time to understand and digest.

Sin Corazón looked at us all. Her eyes were piercing, yet they seemed glazed, as if a dust of some strange perception covered her eyes. As she looked at us, she laughed under her breath, and then she left the circle and moved out toward the west—in a symbolic gesture of death, an ending for her as well. Then she disappeared into the darkness. I would not see her again for some time.

We in the circle stood by the light of the moon, not knowing what to do. Agnes and Ruby, on either side of me, and Twin Dreamers, a few women away, sat down in the dirt. And we all sat down. Jaguar Woman took out her sacred smoke, and we passed it from one of us to the other. We were silent, full of grief for a sister who had lost her way. Yet a voice inside me told me that this was going to be the beginning of a long journey of transformation that might, indeed, be one of the most mysterious of all.

Sin Corazón had been a friend to me, but I had never been able to follow her into these valleys of darkness that she seemed to love so much. So I sat, waited, and watched Jaguar Woman intently. But Jaguar Woman was deep within her own thoughts, deep within her own consternation and wondering. She was not available to us, so I sat in silence and prayed for the spirit of our lost sister.

"What will happen to her?" I whispered to Agnes.

Agnes reached over and held my hand for a moment with her strong fingers.

"It may take her many lifetimes to realize the depth of the decision that she has just made," Agnes said. "There is no telling why the Great Spirit works in such mysterious ways. That is what makes life so powerful a challenge for learning, if only you can see that the forks in the trail are opportunities."

"But, Agnes, she has been banished from one of the greatest sisterhoods that has ever been! What can there be for her except desolation and pain?"

Agnes grinned at me. "Little Wolf, don't get caught in the dream. Don't misunderstand what you are seeing!"

"I don't understand," I said. "How can she turn against us all? She tried to hurt us, steal our power, betray us. Why?"

"Never forget that life is a process of waking up from a long and ancient sleep of the soul. Each of us has to fill up the emptiness inside us in different ways. There is a great hole inside Sin Corazón."

"Is that why she has done what she has done?" I asked.

"Yes." Agnes nodded. "That is why." She placed her hand over my solar plexus, which was tense and hurting. "It is *there* that she is empty. Surely you saw the hole, as we all did."

"Oh, yes," I said.

"That hole is a different kind of hole than one that is created in the heart from loving your family, from attachments to people. Teachers in the world of sorcery would say that if you want personal power without vulnerability, you must forget the past forever and leave those people behind. Our way is different in that there are different kinds of holes, as I see it. Sin Corazón's hole began with heart attachment and became a powerful vulnerability—which is a tragedy. But in another way, it is not a tragedy at all!"

"Why do you say that?" I asked.

Agnes looked at me intently with a glint of merriment in her eyes. "Because Sin Corazón needs powerful messages in her medicine. *She* needs to learn in ways that *you* and I may never dream of. You and I would never choose that trail—not in this lifetime! But who says that we haven't in other lifetimes? Surely we must know those paths, or we could not understand them."

"Agnes, I don't understand how you can be so at ease with all that has just happened."

Agnes gave a big sigh, as if her wolf pup was becoming tiresome. I looked at her, knowing how she felt but still not understanding this dark road that Sin Corazón and so many of her sisters and brothers seemed to be walking at this time in history.

"Yes, it is true," Agnes said. "It is a difficult time. But a difficult time holds deep and profound lessons for each and every one of us. One day, Sin Corazón will have a choice. She can come back—"

"You mean Jaguar Woman would take her back?" I asked in amazement.

"It would depend on the trueness of her heart and what had occurred to bring her back. But I would safely say," Agnes said with a smile, "that this is not over yet. There is much to be learned. And it would not surprise me, Little Wolf, if Sin Corazón approached you."

"Why would you ever say such a thing?" I was aghast.

"Because you are the youngest among us, and she may be foolish enough to think that you are not only the youngest, but the least experienced."

"You mean dumb," I said.

"Well . . . she could think that, and I have a feeling that she may. And if she does, she will approach you to be her ally in some way. Mark my words. We who want to understand more fully get so much more than we bargained for . . ."

"Agnes . . ."

I wanted to continue our conversation, partly to release the pressure that I was feeling in my belly, and also to understand completely what was happening in this circle.

"Agnes, why do women turn against women as they do in my society? When I go home I see it so often! Women who used to love one another somehow get pulled apart, shredded almost. And they are not allies."

With a stick, Agnes drew a circle and then another circle in the sand. The light from the moon shone almost silver off the reflection of the mica chips in the granite and sandstone.

"These," Agnes said, "are shields." She drew four circles representing shields located in the four directions around a larger circle. "Think for a moment that these are your shields. In each direction within you is a male and female shield. When you go to work in a system that is basically patrilineal and patriarchal in its approach, your tendency, whether you are conscious of it or not, is to pick up the male shield. Now this can become very complicated, because your male shield may be part of your Nurturing Mother structure.

"The Great Nurturing Mother is in the north. Death Mother is in the south. Your male shield may be in the Death Mother or the Great Nurturing Mother, depending on whether you use your Great Nurturing Mother energy from a positive or a negative aspect. On the other hand, your male shield could represent the Rainbow Mother in the east or Crazy Woman in the west. If you are an injured Rainbow Mother and you are using a male shield without getting whole first, you're probably going to end up with a male shield that reflects Crazy Woman. And as a result, you are going to move out into the world in a destructive way. Not only will you sabotage your own achievements, but you will also create stress and tension, even chaos, with other people in the workplace and with friends—particularly with other women.

"This is what Sin Corazón has done. She has picked up a male shield that is manifested through Crazy Woman in the west. She's a Rainbow Mother by her essence, but she never healed the dark side of her Rainbow Mother energy. That's why she moved into sorcery. Jaguar Woman tried to send Sin Corazón into the center of her self-wound, which included dark sorcery and reflected all of the things that she needed to learn. But what happened with her husband was a shadow form for things that had happened in her childhood; she did not have the strength or the will to heal—at least not then. But things change every day. That's why I'm saying she may drop that Crazy Woman male shield—at which point she will come back to Jaguar Woman for healing. But if she has not dropped that shield, Jaguar Woman will have nothing to do with her.

"Not that it's incorrect for a woman to hold up a male shield. Far from it. All of the shields are there for your use, but they must give you strength and power. They must not keep you from your true energy. And you must not be wounded when you carry them."

"So are you saying, Agnes—this I never understood clearly—that you have a Rainbow Mother and you have a Great Nurturing Mother within you?"

"Yes," Agnes said.

"And if you are a Great Nurturing Mother, you also have to understand, absorb, and work with respect and infinite care with the dark side of your mother energy, which—if you are a Great Nurturing Mother—includes the Death Mother. And out of the understanding of that energy with the female shields, there is also a male shield counterpart. Is that correct?"

"Yes," she answered.

"So you're saying that if I choose to go into the world with a male shield as a Great Nurturing Mother, healed and whole and have worked through the self-wounds from my earlier experience and have healed those effects on my consciousness, fine. But if I haven't worked with those aspects of myself and I pick up a male shield to go work in the world—to become successful as a writer or whatever—and I have not worked on my stuff"—Agnes smiled at my use of the word *stuff*—"then I would pick up a male shield and it would be filled with Death Mother energy, which is negative and destructive. That's what you're saying?"

"Exactly. And the same goes for the Rainbow Mother in the east, whose dark side is Crazy Woman energy in the west. So Sin Corazón never healed, and she has gone into the male world of sorcery. Not that there isn't a female world of sorcery, but she has chosen a male teacher to work with—partly because that's the energy she seems to work with best at this time in her life. This is not to say that she cannot change."

"So, Agnes, again, how does that apply to women in the world?"

"It applies to *most* women. Most of us need to do so much work on ourselves that it takes a lifetime, sometimes even longer, to get over the difficult or even abusive conditioning we had as children. This is a great challenge, this life today, because there is so much that we need to deal with. Sin Corazón is no different.

"So often you will find that the really talented women you meet, extraordinary women in the universities, in the professions, are expressing new ways of looking at female reality. All the women in the arts today whom you talk about are special in some way. I can perceive the energy field over your societies— it's a very beautiful thing to see. But also," she said, stabbing the stick into the center of the circle, "I see these special women are tormented by what they see and by what they know. Because of that, they isolate in unusual ways. They are set in upon themselves in a way that implodes their energy and sometimes hurts them very badly. Often they are in a lot of pain because they feel misunderstood; the world does not hear them. That is changing, but in a lot of instances it is still, unfortunately, true. Then a woman will pick up her injured negative shield to go out into the male world, and that male shield is not whole. It is full of the Death Mother energy of the south or Crazy Woman energy of the west.

"So, Little Wolf, it is very important to understand those aspects of energy and heal them. Otherwise, you can't do much good in the world. And, unfortunately, the damage that you do can undo all of the good that you are attempting."

I traced the circles that she had drawn in the sand several times, thinking about her words and realizing that there was great wisdom in what she was saying. I knew it was important to see those shields not only as symbols but also as a paradigm for the process of mind. They represent energy forms that we all create and must be responsible for.

But because a shield is an energy form, it can be changed, it can be worked with, and it can be managed. What has always terrified me was finding myself in a situation with an apprentice in which I could not change something for her. Sometimes there is no way to rebuild an energy form because of disease, not only of the body but of the spirit—for example, if someone has lost her will to live or her hope to find truth and beauty.

Sitting there that night, with my circle of sisters, I felt a better understanding. I felt a new hope for Sin Corazón. If she healed, her shields would fully heal as well, and these painful circumstances truly could be changed.

From the other side of the fire and the silver gray plumes of smoke, a slow drumbeat began. We all picked up our drums and accompanied Jaguar Woman and her heartbeat rhythm as she sang and chanted a haunting song about a mother losing her daughter in blood sacrifice to the warriors of the sun.

5

A Sorcerer's Crossroad

"Thank you, my sisters, for joining us tonight. I know that this has been a very long journey for you, but there was no way that we could have done this ceremony without you." Agnes, Ruby, and I walked with Jaguar Woman back to her hut. I looked up at the sky, black with rain-filled clouds on the horizon. The moonlight separated the sky into silvery streaks of light and dark. When we entered the hut, Jaguar Woman lit a kerosene lamp, and we sat around the table together. I continued to look out the window at the moon, shimmering, beautiful, a disk of light in the surrounding darkness. I could not help remembering Sin Corazón and how she had seemed like a black moon in the ceremony that night.

"Jaguar Woman, can you tell us what has happened to Sin Corazón? I know that she was an apprentice of yours, and I loved her when I knew her with you years ago."

Jaguar Woman seemed thoughtful and quiet. Obviously she was experiencing a tremendous amount of sadness. Yet there seemed to be a light of hope in her eyes, as if she knew something that we did not.

"Lynn, it is time, as I know Agnes and Ruby have told you, for you to look deeply into the dark labyrinths of your soul."

"I hope," I said, "I will not end up like Sin Corazon."

Ruby put her hand over mine for a moment. "But there is no way, Little Wolf. You are not anywhere near Sin Corazón—unless—no, that wouldn't happen to you. You would not move into that place of sorcery and evil, unless . . ." Ruby paused.

"Unless what?" I demanded.

"Unless for instance . . ." She rose and walked slowly around the room, placing her fingers just above sacred objects that Jaguar Woman had collected over the years: a small leather bundle, a wrapped blanket tied with thongs. Ruby seemed to stare out the window for a moment, but she was really looking into the interior of her mind. Then she turned to me, in almost a menacing way, and said, "If you were to move into the south direction on the sacred wheel, into a place of nurturing—a place that you have within yourself but don't often use—something very dangerous could happen. You have always picked up the west shield, little one. But now an interesting test is upon you, I think."

I stared at her from my chair. I felt my stomach tighten, my solar plexus beginning to shield against an unknown assault.

"You see, if you moved into the south on the wheel . . . into the little girl? That place where you wanted to be nurtured as a child and were not—particularly by your father!—you become vulnerable. He nurtured you, but he didn't. He, too, was a Rainbow Man. He nurtured the essence of you, but he practically let your body starve. Now if Sin Corazón . . . for instance . . ."

Ruby continued her circular walk around the room. The other women remained sitting and were listening intently.

"If Sin Corazón comes to you . . ."

Jaguar Woman flashed a smile, and then her eyes turned dark as she listened carefully.

"If she comes to you for help, Little Wolf . . . you are going to feel compassion."

"No." I looked at her, shaking my head emphatically no.

"I think it is possible you might feel compassion. Because you know what it is like to lose your way. As a little girl, you lost your way in a forest for a very long time, and there was no one to care for you. In a sense, you were lost in a forest of terror and fear and emotions. Sin Corazón may well come to you and appeal to that child in your south—the south of you—which could mean self-destruction. If you pick up that shield, it will be a most interesting event."

"But Ruby, I have spent all these years being trained as a healer. If my sister comes to me for help, why would I not heal her?"

"Let me ask *you* a question. If an alcoholic came to you and asked you for money for a bottle of booze, and he was in agony and had the DTs, would you give him money?"

"Well . . . no," I said, "because it would only be prolonging his agony."

"Exactly!" she said. Ruby twirled around on her heels, walked out the door, and was lost in the darkness. There was a red-and-blue Guatemalan blanket hanging from a pole at one side of the door. It ruffled in the breeze and swung to the side as she left. I watched that blanket as it moved into a place of stillness behind Ruby.

I looked toward Agnes. "And what about Sin Corazón? Why would she come to me for help?"

"Well, we can speak of that in a moment. At this time, Lynn, what is most important, I think, is to understand what can happen. What is good and evil? What is negative energy and positive energy? These directions and shields mean nothing if they don't serve you, if they don't help you to understand.

"The directions give you a way of thinking, but they are also very real energy forms. Remember that you are sur-rounded by a luminous form of light, a sphere, almost egg shaped, that contains many things. It contains your shields, your energy fields, your luminosity, your ways of approaching the world. There is so much to what you do, and so many wheels of power with different meanings. There is so much to this luminous light that you are. It takes a lifetime to under-stand it all.

"I want you to understand what is happening here. Sin Corazón is an east-west woman like yourself, but very early on, she moved into her opposite, negative side: Crazy Woman in the west of the wheel. She was fascinated by the dark side, by magic.

"Whenever you move toward evil, you cross a line. There is

no question that you make a choice. She made that choice once to go ahead and crossed over—fell over—that line into an abyss. She picked up a male shield, interestingly enough. She could have picked up a female shield, and it could have still been part of Crazy Woman. Instead, she picked up the male aspect—powerful, strong, negative, controlling, active in the world. The female aspect of Crazy Woman would have been quieter, more receptive, more womblike in its ability to accept knowledge and wisdom. Instead, she picked up the spear. She moved forward, active, out into the world. She did terrible things. And throughout the rest of her life, she will pay for them, one by one ... even if today, at this very moment, she moved back into the light and picked up her strong east direction again.

"But you see, if she comes to you for help, for a meeting, most likely she's going to be tricking you. She wants you to move into the south, into that place of compassion-for-the-child. She may come to you as a little girl, wanting you to move into sympathy and vulnerability. Now if you want to take care of her as a mother would, that will throw her into despair. You move into the north, and she'll move into the south to balance you energetically. So, Little Wolf ... something for you to think about!"

I was very indignant. "I would not be caught in such a dance with Sin Corazón."

"Well, we'll see, won't we?" Jaguar Woman smiled. "There is a lot to be learned here, and we have much to do. Just remember, in this dilemma with Sin Corazón, the south represents great danger."

"As Ginevee used to tell you," Agnes put in, "you are close up dead sometimes. What she meant is that sometimes you do not look into all aspects of yourself. It's very important to look at all of your anxieties and impulses. Oftentimes, they lead you into dark places. Darkness does define the light"—Agnes pointed to the sky outside the window—"just as that magnificent black horizon is defined by the light of the moon."

Wanting to know what had happened to Sin Corazón, we all looked toward Jaguar Woman. She thought for a long time, running her fingers over a small stone fetish that she held in her hands.

"I have worked with Sin Corazón for many years. She was fascinated by the dark side of magic. In her work with me, it became very clear that she was exploring that world. But it was inappropriate for me. It is simply not what I do. So I sent her to an old man—a sorcerer in the jungles near here whom I have known most of my life. He is a dark seed with tremendous power. And yes, I threw her into the center of that world. For her, it was sink or swim. For Sin Corazón, this was something that had to be; it was simply part of her soul."

"Remember," Ruby interjected, "this is a life about enlightenment. It is not about happiness or unhappiness. It is about learning. This is what she needed to learn."

"I understand," I said, remembering my vision in Canada of the old man sorcerer.

Ruby rolled her sky blue eyes toward the ceiling as if saying, Oh thank God for that. We all laughed.

"You must remember," Jaguar Woman continued, "Sin Corazón was a householder at the time, married to a man whom she truly believed was her spirit husband. He was not, but no matter what we told her, she would not listen. So when Sin Corazón happily went off to work with the old sorcerer, her husband, unfortunately, found his way to another woman's bed and left with her. This was something that we did not know about until much later, when Sin Corazón was at a crossroads in her training. Someone unwittingly went to her and told her what had happened, not knowing the sorcerer's crossings and the way of our world of power. Because of that, the timing, and so much of Sin Corazón's life in the past—abuse and very painful activities that went on in her childhood—she simply lost her way. She went into a kind of grief beyond anything I have ever witnessed. Something about her husband had simply stolen her self-respect, obviously, or she would not have been taken in by the old man as well.

"Remember, Black Wolf, you cannot compare one person to another, or one person's grief to another's. What rammed her down into hell may have only shaken you to your roots. You could have recovered; she could not. And with revenge, with envy, with jealousy, she went headlong into the world of dark sorcery. Because we didn't know this for a time, because we didn't know what had happened and we weren't paying attention, because I was busy with other apprentices, I let her go to whatever teachings she needed to find. She needed to be free of me to do whatever she needed. Her guardian spirits came to me in ceremony, and then I went to her. But by then, she considered herself stronger than me—certainly my equal in the world of power. We circled each other and left each other alone. It was not a confrontation, but it was absolutely a break of the bonding that we had had all those years. Because she didn't care about her life anymore, she became very dangerous. A result of that was the ceremony you took part in tonight."

For a long time we all pondered what Jaguar Woman had told us. Finally, I broke the silence.

"Jaguar Woman, my heart goes out to you. Losing an apprentice in this way is a very painful event, I know. What confuses me is how someone so powerful, who has such ability and has worked with you a long time, could turn toward evil. She knows the difference between right and wrong. Forget moralistic judgment. She understands the energy lines that lead toward the source of power. How could her husband— her spirit husband, even—throw her? How could she lose it so totally?"

Jaguar Woman looked at me with a slight smile on her lips.

"Yes, this is painful, Black Wolf. It is a wonderment to me as well that she could have been so thrown by that event. I am saddened, not for me, but because I see the pain Sin Corazón is heading for, and I cannot remove it for her. Maybe her destiny in this lifetime is simply to submerge into the depths of evil.

Maybe she chose her husband to do this, maybe it was an agreement. Many times it is that way. It is not for us to judge, to know, or even perhaps to try to understand. We can only take responsibility for our own relationship with power."

With that, Jaguar Woman stood up. It was obvious that our conversation was over for the evening.

We were all very tired. Jaguar Woman led us in through a hallway to another hut, where our hammocks were stretched, ready for us. Agnes, Ruby, and I gratefully prepared for sleep.

6

Stealing Power

The next evening we sat again with Jaguar Woman and continued our discussion about Sin Corazón.

"Jaguar Woman, we've talked a lot about darkness," Agnes said. "This banishment ceremony has troubled me to the core of my spirit."

"It deeply saddens me also," Jaguar Woman said.

"Jaguar Woman," I said, "forgive my ignorance, but what is it that Sin Corazón actually did? What were her evil ways that you speak about? I really have never heard the stories, other than just that she was steeped in darkness."

Jaguar Woman got up from the table, took a deep breath, and walked over to the window to look out at the moonlight reflecting off the broad leaves outside in her back portal area. Finally, after several minutes of thoughtfulness, she turned to us.

"It is difficult to explain how someone like this thinks every day about only herself, about how to take other people's power and make it her own. The stories of how she would use men, for instance, were many. She would steal their power."

"What do you mean, steal their power?" I asked.

"As I have said, Sin Corazón's name in English means No Heart, or Woman Without Heart. Of course in our world of power her name means One of Great Heart. Odd, isn't it? Her name even speaks of evil. She would literally leave men empty shells of what they had been."

"But how does one do that?" I said. "Don't they have a choice?"

"Well, yes and no. She had the ability to find someone's vulnerability. If a man fell in love with her, which so often they did because she is so beautiful, she would drain their power through sex and leave them half-mad, or she would find the vulnerability within their love. For instance, maybe he would need to have an ordered life. She would quickly find that addiction to order, which was basically a weakness, and prey upon it, creating an illness out of it within that person. In other words, if it was not a weakness before, she made sure that it became a weakness, far beyond the vulnerability it was in the first place.

"She would suddenly become unavailable. She would create emotional chaos within the other person. She would say that she was going to do something with him, meet him somewhere, and then not show up, or change her mind, or in some way start driving that person crazy. She also had the ability to enter their dreams. She would go past their guardians without thought. You would say, 'Well, someone can't do that unless you allow them in.' That's true. But when you are in love, you will allow almost anything in. That's how things happen. She used the weaknesses of men and women as a kind of control. She initiated trust and then betrayed them. She was an energy thief.

"Now, Sin Corazón worked solitarily. A large group of people was never her interest. She liked moving alone, completely alone. That's why falling in love with another person is so incredibly difficult for her. That's why it would be hard for her to bond with another person, as in marriage.

"I'll tell you a specific story. She was in Montana, where a young man seduced her, and in her anger and revenge toward men, she took his life's spirit, almost as if she sucked his blood away. She left him absolutely mad, wandering in the wilderness, not remembering who he was or why he was alive. When they found him, it was as if a vampire had taken his life force and left him the shell of the person he had been. Years and years later he did recover. Now you might say, 'He made the first move,' and that is true. If they had been in a gunfight, he had certainly made the first draw. But that is her strange power and her ability. Many of the things that Sin Corazón was involved in and did, I know nothing about. All I can tell you is that she had the power to manipulate, to use, to completely turn situations around for her own bidding, but when she did that, it was never for anyone else's good but always for her personal gain. She very definitely made deals, so to speak, with the guardians of the dark netherworld. That is who she is."

"Are there any other stories you can tell us so we can understand her better?"

"One of her favorite things to do," Jaguar Woman said, "was to become friends with a woman, find out who her best friends were, and sooner or later those friends were completely angry with one another and broken apart forever. She would do it in many ways, mainly, again, by preying upon their weaknesses, finding the soft heart of fear and magnifying that completely. That is the kind of woman she is. She will turn the members of a family against one another: daughter against mother, mother against daughter, father against son."

"But why would she act in such a hurtful, destructive way?" I asked.

"Because of her early relationships. I wasn't going to speak of this, but she was abandoned as a baby on the steps of an orphanage. Then she was adopted. Her stepfather beat her and molested her. When she married, she mated like a wolf—for life. When her husband then deserted her, she turned against the Sisterhood, somehow, even though she loved all of us once. That love was a fine line that became hate for her. A person like that can do great damage."

"I hesitate to say this, but I know of many women and men who behave in a similar way," I said, amazed that it was true.

"Yes." Jaguar Woman came close to me, looking into my eyes. "But I will bet you that those women and men create chaos and pain out of greed and envy, right? The chaos that is created is left hanging like smoke on the wind, right?"

"Yes, you're right."

"That is bad enough, but Sin Corazón gathers that smoke and blows it into castles of energy for her own use. She stores that energy. That is the difference. The old sorcerer trained her well, and now he owns her will."

"Her will?"

"Yes, he took her as a kind of energy slave. When you become an apprentice or a healer to one of us, you move toward enlightenment. His way is of darkness, and he has bound her will to his own. In the darkness they are twin spirits. But I believe she is trying to pull away and doesn't know how."

Jaguar Woman thought for some time. "I believe that only love could heal her now, but she would have to be in love to create the gateway for light to enter her soul."

"Fat chance of that happening." Ruby snorted. She pushed aside her chair and headed for her hammock. "This is all too much for an old blind Indian woman."

We all laughed, relieved to change the subject and head for sleep. It had been another long day.

7
The Shaman's Jewel

Sin Corazón fumbled in the semi-darkness of Jaguar Woman's hut. She knew she had only a short time before her former teacher would return. It had been several days since the horrible banishment ceremony, and she was still very angry.

Many years ago, Jaguar Woman had shown her the hiding place for the Shaman's Jewel. Now, Sin Corazón's fingers, unreasonably stiff and awkward, grabbed at the layers of ceremonial blankets covering a tiny door in a back corner of the room. This was where Jaguar Woman kept her hidden altar and medicine bags. Sin Corazón was unaccustomed to such extraordinary stress. Usually she was afraid of nothing, but something about what she was doing filled her with terror. Because of that, she was off her center, and she knew it. She straightened up for a moment, took several deep breaths, and placed her palm over her solar plexus, trying to regain her composure. Maybe she should leave and return at another time? But if she had the Shaman's Jewel, she had everything.

Sin Corazón began to ransack the hut. The Shaman's Jewel was not in its customary sacred place. Furious, she looked in every crevice, in the back of every drawer, tearing the bedclothes away from their pile waiting for winter. At last, in her whirlwind of desire and fervent searching, she realized that Jaguar Woman had suspected that she would come here. She hissed through her teeth with anger. She held up her hands, trying to move into her place of power so that she could feel the stone. An ordinary theft would have taken only moments, but the hiding place was not revealed. Sin Corazón was in a fury.

Then she felt the nearness of her teacher. She knew that she must flee instantly. In a moment of spontaneity and misplaced regret, she reached inside her own medicine bag that hung from her neck and took out a many-faceted garnet sphere that Jaguar Woman had given her as an object of power, long ago. She wanted her teacher to know that she had been there, to know that she was challenging her. But as she laid the garnet down in the center of the table, she felt a moment of trepidation, a contraction in her belly and in her heart. In the madness of Sin Corazón's pain and relentless selfishness, she saw clearly, for one fleeting second, that she was asking for help. Strangely, this was the only way that she could reach out toward Jaguar Woman; the only way that the depth of her poisoned being could find a voice and be heard.

She laid the garnet down gently, soundlessly, and with care. There was even a moment of love. And then, whirling like a cloud of black smoke from a dying fire, she spun through the doorway and was lost in the night.

8
Gateway into the Dream

Before dawn, Agnes and I received a message that we were to meet with Jaguar Woman back at her village.

Several days before, Agnes and I had traveled to a village near Uxmal to visit Zoila and José. Almost never had we received messages of this kind. Always in our world of dreaming we would simply dream or become aware of an energy pulling us, and we would simply be somewhere at a given time designated by no one, and the person we needed to see would be there. This was different, and, again, it was urgent.

Agnes looked at me with her eyebrows raised and shook her head with a smile. "Let's be on our way," she said to me, handing me my medicine bag.

We were both glad to return. Jaguar Woman lived in a sleepy little town near Palenque in the Yucatán of southern Mexico. The village knew there was a woman of power in their midst, but to them she was a *curandera*, a woman who worked with herbs and had an uncanny way of disappearing for long periods of time and showing up unexpectedly. She had raised a family in this village, and her husband of over forty years had moved into the spirit world a long time ago.

Jaguar Woman answered the blue-painted door. Her white hair was pulled back in a knot at the nape of her neck. She wore, as she often did, a white cotton dress embroidered with brilliantly colored threads in flowered patterns the way they do in the villages of the Yucatán. She wore large silver earrings that dangled. A smile crinkled the corners of her eyes. She was a beautiful woman. I was always in awe of her, not unlike my feelings for Ruby, because I never knew what Jaguar Woman was going to do. Her house had stone floors and wattle and daub walls, with windows opening out onto the garden and corn pasture beyond. The jungle had been cut back around the area of her small farm. It smelled of earth and humidity and sunshine and exquisite health.

I heard a cough and then a giggle from the shadows. I whirled around to see Ruby standing beside me, smiling at my instant sense of foreboding. I was happy to see Ruby, as always, but if she and Jaguar Woman were together again, I knew that something big was afoot. Most likely I would be at the center of some teaching activity having to do with a flaw in my own shamanic abilities. I took a deep breath and gave Jaguar Woman the gourd that I had painted for her. I had brought nothing for Ruby.

"May I give Ruby these?" I asked Jaguar Woman, pointing to the bananas in the gourd.

Jaguar Woman smiled. Taking them out of the gourd herself with her strong hands, she handed them to me.

"Ruby, I am so happy to see you. I thought you had gone north."

Everyone laughed. Agnes poked Ruby in the ribs. Jaguar Woman put her arm around my shoulders as we walked over the threshold, my eyes adjusting to the dim light of her two-room house. Her doors were open to a portal along the back of the house. The sleeping room was off to the right. Through an open doorway I could see the sleeping hammocks hung between the walls. Despite the smiles of Jaguar Woman and Ruby, I could sense there was concern, an urgency in the air.

Jaguar Woman brought out some green drinks for each of us, set them on the round wooden table in the room. A pleasant breeze lifted the corners of the white cotton tablecloth. Each of us sat down in expectation. In silence Jaguar Woman took from the medicine bag hanging around her neck a many-faceted object about an inch in diameter and placed it in the center of the table.

It was a dark, red-colored stone. Ruby picked it up and rolled it around in the palm of her hand. Then Ruby passed it to Agnes, who felt it for several moments in her left hand before handing it to me. It looked like a many-faceted garnet. The other two women seemed as confused as I was. We all looked at Jaguar Woman for an explanation.

"That *is* a garnet," she said. "It has been used in ceremony for many years. As you can feel, it has much power. But nothing has as much power and history of ceremony with our circle as the Shaman's Jewel, the star ruby that is at the center of our power circle."

We all nodded in agreement.

"To get to why I called you back—as you know, this is all highly unusual, and I honor you all for being close to me with your intent. As you know, the Shaman's Jewel," she said, "is our precious, sacred power object. Several nights ago, Sin Corazón attempted to steal it."

We all gasped in astonishment. I watched the anger momentarily flash across Jaguar Woman's face. I could feel the tension in the air.

"What happened?" I finally asked.

"I was at a ceremony late into the night at the world altar down by the old sun temple near the ruins of Palenque. I came back early to meet with my daughter. When I arrived, I felt tremendous dissension and a scattering of energy, and I knew that something was wrong. You know how well hidden the Shaman's Jewel is. So does Sin Corazón. Not really believing that she might ever try to steal it, I still felt the need to move the Shaman's Jewel to another place. Sin Corazón ransacked the house because the jewel wasn't in its old familiar place. I dreamed her, and much to my surprise, she wanted the Shaman's Jewel not for itself, but because the jewel tells where the seven clay pots rest in their secret cave. She knows of the sacred diagram on the floor of that temple at Palenque. She knows of the hidden doors that lead to that chamber where the star wheels are hidden. With the Shaman's Jewel, she can go into those vaults and discover the location of the seven clay pots. That is what she is after, and it is most dangerous that she is thinking in this way. Although I am asking your counsel, I believe that it is time that we attempt to heal Sin Corazón because I feel in my heart that she, by making such an aggressive movement toward our most sacred object, is asking for help."

"She'll get helped, all right," said Ruby, a moment of fury in her eyes. "I'll help her into the next universe. She'll be so far away she'll never find her way back." Then she laughed, as if making light of her statement. But I wasn't sure that she was kidding.

Agnes shook her head. "Maybe you're right, Jaguar Woman. But I would be very, very careful, because I'm beginning to wonder if maybe she's just too far gone."

"We are never too far gone," Jaguar Woman said.

"How did you know for sure it was Sin Corazón?" I asked.

Jaguar Woman held out the garnet. "I gave her this garnet as part of her medicine bag, as part of her tools for healing, long years ago. She left it in the center of my table. She wanted me to know that she had been here."

"Why would she do this? In the cities, you expect someone to rob you, you expect people to be envious and greedy. But how could someone who has worked with you, Jaguar Woman, ever conceive that you would not destroy her for infringing in such a blasphemous way?"

"Everything in this life, Black Wolf, is part of the teaching of spirit. If you come upon evil in your lifetime, you are filled with a longing for the end of that evil, for light, for something better. But oftentimes, when you see that evil, you don't know how to get rid of it. You don't know how to heal it, so you try to get out of its way, to move out of its influence into something better and more comfortable and peaceful. But even that can be a tall order when you are talking about the war that goes on within a special human being like Sin Corazón, given the power that the old sorcerer has over her. Even though she has discarded all she knows of goodness, she is crying out for help. I am angry at the way that she has done it because it puts the entire Sisterhood in a state of risk, and so, my decision to move in an aggressive way to heal her."

"And how do you think that can be done?" Agnes asked.

"You do not heal through a process of anger. When I see people with placards marching through the streets, screaming and fighting for a better way, I know that their fight will be endless and useless, because only love can heal that kind of sickness."

"So what you're saying, Jaguar Woman, is that you want to approach Sin Corazón through love?"

Ruby smiled, rapping her knuckles on the table, obviously moving into the thoughts of Jaguar Woman where I could not follow. It was as if the three women moved through the gateway of sunlight streaming through the window. An arrow of light reflected off the garnet in the center of the table, where Jaguar Woman had carefully placed it. I could feel the women energetically moving toward me to take me with them, through the gateway into the dream world, where higher counsel is found, where higher aspects and pieces of ourselves are found, where knowledge and wisdom reside in abundance.

As I felt them encircle me, I moved my consciousness into my dream body. Carefully and with intent, I remembered a dream from the night before, a kind of déjà vu of what was happening at this moment. Following along the pathways that the dream had provided for me, I moved with my sisters into the energy field of the sacred dream. As we did so, I sensed a shift in the reality around me, as if I were moving from photographic positive into negative, as if colors were shifting into more black and white. Things were slower, as if I had become heavy. My body fell away, and my spirit moved into light with my teachers.

We continued to talk, the four of us. Jaguar Woman asked me to hold the position of the south, the position of trust and innocence, of childlike emotion. She asked Ruby to handle the east, the wise old keeper of wisdom, the coyote among us. She herself took the west, the sacred dream, rebirth and transformation of all that lives. Agnes sat in the position of spirit, strength, and prayer in the north. "Love is here, in the center of the table," Jaguar Woman said, her voice sounding very far away.

I felt that I would slip back through that gateway into the reality of every day, but I hung on with my intent for dear life. I was able to sit with my sisters in council in a different way than I ever had before.

"Julio," said Ruby, from her position in the east. "Perhaps Julio."

She bounced this off, as if the idea was a ball of light that landed in front of us.

"Ah," Jaguar Woman said, "yes, Julio. So strong. So handsome, and so powerful in the ways of love and healing. And he has never met his match. He has always used women and hurt them by leaving them. What an interesting idea!"

To me Julio had always been a mysterious messenger of power. He seemed to appear out of nowhere with extraordinary information and then disappear suddenly without a word. He was handsome and very seductive to women.

Once, a few years ago, I was at Agnes's cabin. I came out of the smokehouse, not knowing Julio was there, and felt two strong hands grab me, silencing my yell of surprise. He carried me around to the back of the shed. In front of the cabin was a large brown bear and her cub.

Bears can be very dangerous when they think someone might hurt their young. I watched as Julio, tall and lean, approached the bear. He spoke to her in a Mayan dialect with a gentle voice, telling her it was dangerous for her to be there and for her to leave.

The bear stood on her hind legs and faced Julio, snarling and swinging her paws in defiance. He stood his ground and kept on speaking to her with no fear. Slowly she dropped to all fours and ran with her cub into the forest. I learned later that Julio has great powers with animals, and bear is one of his medicines.

Julio had come in and out of our lives, taking on the names of other people, but I always knew that he was Julio, a member of Zoila's family. Sin Corazón had been married to Zoila's cousin. Julio was another member of her family, a powerful man, close to Sin Corazón's age.

"But he can never marry or be committed to a woman," I said. "It is not his way."

"Yes," Agnes interjected, "but there are many kinds of commitment in the worlds of power in personal relationships. They could love, and they could heal each other."

"Does he work in dark sorcery as well?" I asked, surprised.

"No," Jaguar Woman said. "His healing has to do with trust and his heart."

"So if they are attracted to each other," Agnes said, "it may be perfect." She reached out her left hand, as if she were grabbing hold of something. Her eyes were closed. She began to tug at the air, as if it were filled with substance, then reached up her right hand and began to pull, as if grasping a cord or a line of some kind. Tremendous light emanated from inside her, as if her body were filled with tiny crystals.

"Agnes," I said, "your light is so extraordinary. What are you doing?" I wanted to know what she was doing because I wanted to do it myself, to help her.

"I am bringing the light of love into my bloodstream, and as I do this, I am healing what you would call the immune system within my body. It is the secret to our longevity, because as we light the pathways of light energy and force in our bodies, our immune systems become more powerful to fight disease. It is the secret of many ancient societies and civilizations that have gone before us. It is one of the great secrets that you will come upon in the seven clay pots. This is happening to me because I wish to show you what can be yours. It strengthens the balance of power within every cell of my body so that only truth can live within me. It is time for the seven clay pots to be revealed to you, Little Wolf. And it is time to heal our fallen sister, and Julio is a good choice. If anyone can absorb her dark reflection and transform it into light, it is he. But she will have to choose him of her own free will. And he must also choose her. It can only be that way. It is law."

I was filled with awe with the reflectioin of brilliance in the room. The room had been very hot before we had come in. It was now very cool and silent, except for the crackling of light around Agnes. All of us sat in silence and respect.

"Then let it be so," Jaguar Woman stated. With these words, she engulfed me again, along with the other women, in an energy field that seemed to suck itself around me like flowing water moving around a rock, back into the gateway of light, back into the room of everyday reality.

We sat at the table for a long time, silently adjusting our consciousness and bodies back to where we had originally been. I felt very lightheaded and was suddenly very hungry.

After some time Jaguar Woman got up and brought a papaya and some tortillas and cheese back to the table. With deft slices of the knife, she cut open the papaya and gave us slices of cheese. We ate together silently, each deep in our own thoughts. A state of bliss surrounded us all.

Agnes, Ruby, and I returned to the North in the next few days. As we traveled we spoke of our experience in the Yucatán. Agnes also revealed to me that we would soon be traveling to the sacred cave that is the home of the seven clay pots. I was filled with anticipation and wonder for what lay before me.

9
The Seven Clay Pots

As Agnes and I climbed the high stone walls of the foothills, I could sense a stillness, as if we were approaching the center of a powerful vortex of energy. The sheer face of sandstone was striated with red iron oxides; it appeared as though the cliffs over the centuries had been weeping. There was a widening in the trail, and Agnes took a turn and suddenly disappeared. I followed her quickly and realized that she simply had walked around a large boulder.

There was a flat place in the boulder, and she was feeling it with her hands. She looked up at the sun; it was about three o'clock.

"Perfect," she muttered to herself. She placed her hands on the boulder, and asked me to help her. "Push," she ordered.

"Push?" I asked, looking at the size of the enormous boulder, thinking full well that we could never move it.

"Push," she reiterated.

As we did, I realized that the stone must have been carved on the bottom in a certain way. Actually, it rolled fairly easily, considering its enormity and weight. The stone kind of wobbled and then settled quickly, but the mountain of rocks opened to reveal a hidden passageway.

Agnes took me by the hand and had me stand on a flat piece of what looked like slate. A ridge about two inches high had been carved into the slate, and she asked me to put my toes up against the ridge. I was amazed by all of this, speechless, thinking that we had just gone for a walk up into these foothills to look out across the vast expanse of plains.

"Put your feet there," she ordered. "Pay attention," she snapped.

I put my toes up against the ridge, realizing this was a very important moment, although I didn't understand exactly what was happening. Again, Agnes looked up at the sun.

Walking first around to my right side, she knelt down in the dirt, as if calibrating something, and then walked around to my shadow, which was wavering off to my side.

"Stand still," she barked.

She placed a design at the end of my shadow, making it almost like a clock, and made seven marks in the dirt, with one hand of the clock moving through the center of my shadow, pointing directly at the first of the seven marks.

"Yes," Agnes said, "as it should be." She came over and gave me a quick hug.

"What's happening, Agnes?"

"I am reading your shadow," she said.

"Is this where the seven clay pots are?" My heart was thumping against my ribs with excitement.

"Before you enter the cave, it is important, essential, that we arrive at a certain time. In the process of reading your shadow, I then know which pot is to be revealed to you."

"But if you enter at a certain time, it would always say the same pot," I said.

"No," she said. "There are other factors I'll explain to you, and that has to do with the placement of the seven marks. All you need to know now is that you are to see the first pot."

"You mean the pots are really in this cave?" I asked incredulously.

"They have been here for centuries. When an apprentice, one among us, reaches a certain place in her evolvement, the pots are revealed to her. And I must tell you," she said, "this is the first time I know of that an apprentice has been given the first pot. So I am very excited."

"As am I," I said. I was so excited that my thoughts were

tumbling over one another in my mind, and I was almost speechless.

Then Agnes took some water in her mouth from a canteen and sprayed it over the area for an honoring of spirit, for a blessing of the spirit of place. Using cedar, she smudged me and herself and made an offering to the keeper of the cave.

I had brought nothing, so I took a strand of my hair and laid it there in front of the cave and said prayers and asked that the keeper of the cave stand up for me and take notice, protect us, guard the cave while we were inside, and keep us safe and secret.

The inside of the cave was as black as a raven. I followed Agnes, hanging on to her. The floor of the cave felt incredibly smooth, almost slippery. Then, as my eyes became accustomed to the darkness and using my ability to *see* in darkness, a deep red light surrounded us. In my *seeing* training, when practicing the gait of power, I had always been aware of a red light, so I wasn't sure if that's what was happening or if there was actually a red glow inside the cave.

As we made one spiral curve down into the earth, we came to a large cavern, vaulted high and round like a kiva. There was light from a recess cut out of the ceiling off to one side. Agnes lit a lantern that she had carried with her.

Suddenly the cavern was ablaze with dancing light.

In the flickering light, I saw that the clay pots were arranged along a large indentation or *nicho* halfway up the wall, set way back, I assumed, for protection. The cave was obviously ceremonial with lines of yellow, red-ocher, blue, on the floor. The designs, as I walked over them carefully, stepping in between the lines so as not to harm them in any way, seemed to be an astrological map of a galaxy.

Agnes sat on the stone shelf and allowed me to examine the cave carefully. She said nothing for a long time. I looked at a configuration of seven stars situated in the universal floor sky that I stood upon. I turned to Agnes.

"This is the seven sister Pleiades, is it not?" I asked.

"Yes, it seems to be so."

"And what does this all mean, Agnes? Why is it etched into the floor this way?"

"Because all knowledge comes from somewhere. Many people would disagree with that, but when the knowledge was given to us, it was perfect, and it made total sense. There was never any room within the teachings for misunderstanding, even for discussion. It was simple, pure truth." She laughed. "That is why it's so difficult for people to bring it into the sacred circle of their own dream. Because it is so simple."

"And the clay pots," I asked, "what does it all mean?"

"Well," Agnes said, "perhaps you need to see for yourself."

"You mean that I get to look into the clay pots? And you say that there are writings there?"

"Yes," Agnes said. "Throughout history, only the women in the Sisterhood, at least to my knowledge, have been allowed to read the teachings in these pots. As it has been told to me by my teachers, they hold the keys to this level and realm of reality—human life as we know it. But also, the pots' manuscripts reveal the connections among the peoples who have been born onto this earth, the relationship of physicalness and spirit, the basis for what we have always called universal shamanism, and the relationship of you to your own universe.

"When you walked into the cave, you noticed that I was observing your shadow." Agnes stood up. "Because your shadow reads in a certain way, I want you to stand over here.

"This is the place of the sacred zero, the place of power for the Zero Chiefs of the Mayan, which are the ancient teachings of the Mayans that are still part of our own teachings, part of the sacred count of life, of the universe, of all that lives.

"When you stand at the place of the sacred zero, you open yourself to new knowledge and new beginnings in your journey toward wisdom."

Agnes went to the shelf and very, very carefully she placed her hands on the first pot. The simple petroglyphic designs on the pot looked to me like renderings of ceremonies, animals, deer, bear, and elk. The pot was large, yet small enough for her to hold in her arms. Sliding it off the shelf, she came over and placed it on the symbol of the sacred zero representing everything that is and the sacredness of nothingness. The pot fit perfectly on the spot, as if it had been designed to be there, as I'm sure it was.

Agnes and I sat on either side of the pot with our hands on her, because I felt that the pot was very female, ready to give birth, ready to share her knowledge with us. The pot was of cool, smooth, burnished clay, one of the most beautiful pots I have ever seen, flawless, not a chip. What a museum would do to get their hands on this pot! I thought.

Then I wondered at the unusualness of the design.

"Agnes, this doesn't appear, really, to be Native American design."

The shape of the pot was typically Native American. The odd designs, which reminded me of Greek or Etruscan vases, were not.

"Is this possibly a Viking ship, Agnes? Look at this."

She looked at it in wonderment.

"It looks to me like a flat boat with shields and a sail," I said.

"Yes," she said, "it looks like it, doesn't it?"

We must have perused the outside of that pot for an hour, it was so beautiful. Then there was a cover to the pot. It rested on a small lip on the inside. Agnes removed it. Inside was a long scroll made out of something I could not identify, either a very strong paper or pressed leather, I wasn't sure. What had worried me the most is that it would have somehow disintegrated into powder, but obviously the people who had written these manuscripts had thought about that a long time ago. They obviously had the knowledge to create something that was seemingly indestructible.

Unrolled, the scroll was about three feet in length and covered with designs and writing. The writing was in an archaic kind of English, using words I could barely recognize because of the old spellings. Interspersed among the sentences were symbols that looked like Sanskrit.

"What is this, Agnes? Why is this in English and not in a native tongue?"

"Because," Agnes said, "native languages were really not written. Three hundred years ago there was a woman in the Sisterhood whom we called a woman of words—not unlike yourself, except that she used the magic of words. The words themselves became entities of life and spirit to her, as they are to you. But for her, words would have sounds and a voice, and they would speak to her as I am speaking to you.

"They would talk of their meaning and speak of their depth and their power to her. They would animate right off of the page. She was a translator, and one of the greatest ones that has ever been part of our circle. These scrolls are ancient in origin."

She took another scroll out of the pot and opened it.

"This is the original scroll," she said.

I looked at it very carefully. The language reminded me of the Norwegian that I had known as a child, but it was still different.

"I could swear this is Sanskrit," I said. "What is it doing in this part of the world?"

I was dumbfounded, wishing with all my heart and soul that I was a linguist and could understand these things more deeply.

"It doesn't matter," Agnes said, "because it is all here. All you need to know will be given to you. Now, about three hundred years ago," she continued, "this woman came into the caves and translated the scrolls, and she did a fine job. She understood perfectly what these scrolls had to give us, so what you have there before you is her translation.

"What I want you to do, my daughter, is to write this out for yourself, for no other eyes. There are certain things that you can reveal, certain things that you can speak of to your people. I will let you know what those things are, but for now, you copy that, because we will need it for the work we are going to be doing."

"What does Sin Corazón have to do with this?" I suddenly remembered my journey with the dark sister.

"We will speak of her this evening," Agnes said, looking up at the waning light coming through the crevice in the vaulted ceiling. "Now we must leave,"

"Leave? What are you talking about? I thought we were going to begin writing."

"It is law, Little Wolf. We cannot spend the night, so we must leave now. But we will return soon, when you find the key. It's up to you."

"What do you mean by 'the key'? I thought—"

"You thought wrong. There is one more thing we must hear from you. You will know when it happens. Now we must go."

We did a brief ceremony. Before I knew it, we were outside the cave and covering our tracks with a branch of mesquite.

10

The Twisted Hair: An Introduction to Jaguar Woman's Story

A year had gone by since we had been together. Agnes, Ruby, and I had returned to the Yucatán for our solstice ceremony with the Sisterhood. All of us were eager to use the occasion to hear about Sin Corazón and Julio as well.

After several days of ceremonies, Jaguar Woman gathered us together in her house, telling us she had something important to share.

Agnes sat on the floor, her back against the adobe wall of the house. I sat on Jaguar Woman's blue-painted chair. Ruby sat in another plain wooden rocking chair, and Jaguar Woman, her hair twisted in a knot on the top of her head, began to circle the room.

"I have a long story to share with you," she finally said. "For you, Lynn, because you need to learn a new way of storytelling, I will relate this story as if it happened to other people. I am in the story, but I will remove my self-importance and speak of myself as Jaguar Woman. Do you understand me?"

"Yes," I answered.

"It is the story of Sin Corazón and Julio. It is a sorcerer's love story, and for each of you it will mean something different."

Jaguar Woman began to move her hands and fingers in an undulating manner to accentuate the words that she spoke. As she began moving right into the scenario and the drama that Julio and Sin Corazón had lived through, she seemed to have a way of bringing the words to life so that our minds were filled with color and sound and imagination to match the delicacy and the care that Jaguar Woman was taking in relating the story to us. It was clear that she wanted us to hear this story with every nuance, with every subtle aspect, because we had been part of the banishment ceremony and because we were part of the sacred circle. Each of our lives belonged to every other woman within that circle. It was part of our initiation, part of the wisdom and the knowledge that we took on as members of the Sisterhood of the Shields, that wherever our trails led, each and every one of these women could follow with us or not, as they chose. It was important that we know and share the color, the texture, and the fragrance of the lives that we were experiencing. Jaguar Woman in her ability as a Twisted Hair, a teller of tales and stories for the education of the spirit, began to tell us this extraordinary tale.

With each segment of this story, Jaguar Woman seemed capable of bringing that landscape of emotions and experience deep into my heart. It was as if each of us were alone in the room with Jaguar Woman, with our own interpretations, our own wonder at how love can transform a life into pain or joy. We each experienced this story in our own way.

I

Long crooked shadows fell across Sin Corazón's path as she ran through the jungle. Her body felt hot, though her skin was ice cold in the sultry damp heat of the evening. She ran and ran, but she came to nothing—only darkness descending as the shards of light, the pieces of illumination that no longer touched her, began to disappear.

Wrapped in her grief for her lost husband, she flung herself facedown onto the moist earth. She felt the hot, weighted air on her back. The ramparts of orchids and sweet-smelling honeysuckle had become foreign weeds no longer tempting her senses with joy. Surely as if a vampire had sucked the last blood from her heart, her spirit flowed out with her soundless screams and down and down, and her silent voice became a turning, coiled serpent in an invisible mist far below her. Pain was closing over her in an impenetrable shroud that burned her identity away. All that was left inside her was food, now, for the huge sucking mouth that began to devour her innards with hate. She felt cold and slimy now. There was no love for her—there never had been, and never again would she trust in the gentle sweetness of a caress. Her bones felt loose and disconnected from her substance. There were no tears now, no understanding, no remorseless craving for goodness or light. Only the darkness felt like new flesh as her body was refashioned to its hideous rebirth with each shuddering breath. Only in her heart was there a vicious longing, an unfathomable abyss of emptiness that would never again be filled.

II

The hut was dark inside when Jaguar Woman quietly slipped in through the door and squatted down so as not to be seen. She watched Sin Corazón wildly rummaging through her sacred things, looking for the Shaman's Jewel.

Fortunately, Jaguar Woman had moved it again. She reached through a hidden place in the wall and grasped the bag that held the Shaman's Jewel. She brought it out and held it to her forehead and to her heart. Then she stood and moved toward a stream of moonlight coming in through the window, bright and intense.

Sin Corazón suddenly stopped her wild fumbling search, knowing instantly what a fool she had been to come back here. She turned, whirling around like a dervish to face her long-lost teacher. Jaguar Woman said nothing. She held the Shaman's Jewel up in the light of the moon. It threw prismatic colors of lavender and silver around the adobe walls, flashing into Sin Corazón's eyes. Jaguar Woman reached out and grabbed Sin Corazón by the hair, yanking her with a grip as strong as iron. Sin Corazón, powerful as she was, knew that she was no match for her teacher. She stood in pain, with her head twisted. Jaguar Woman turned her to face the Shaman's Jewel, which she held in the light.

"Look into the Shaman's Jewel, Sin Corazón. Look carefully for the truth, for the power, for what you seek.

At first Sin Corazón's eyes were closed. Jaguar Woman yanked her until her scalp bled. Sin Corazón opened her eyes and stared into the jewel, into the vortex of energy held within its facets. Stricken by what she saw, she gasped, and her body relaxed. Jaguar Woman did not let go of her but almost supported her with her body, leaning slightly against her.

"Look into the light," Jaguar Woman ordered her once again. "And remember who you are, lost one, who has gone so far away from home. It is time. I know why you have come here, dark sister, so I meet you halfway. Look well into the light and be healed."

Long moments went by as Sin Corazón stared unblinking into the brilliant stream of light. Jaguar Woman could sense the shift within Sin Corazón's body. With her ability to understand the energetic connections within a person's body, Jaguar Woman made well-placed thumps in several places on Sin Corazón's spine. The younger woman suddenly went rigid, then spun around with terror in her eyes, stared at Jaguar Woman briefly, and then fled from the room, back into the darkness outside, and disappeared into the night.

Jaguar Woman knew that her mission had been accomplished. Once again the Shaman's Jewel had performed its magic of power and light. Sin Corazón's energy had been shifted, and perhaps it would only be a matter of time before she left the old sorcerer forever. His grasp on her had been weakened, and that dark energy could snap back into its proper abode within the world of the old sorcerer in the jungle.

It would take time, though, for Sin Corazón to adjust to the new energy flow within her body. Ever so slowly she would begin to see beauty again in the world. Replacing the Shaman's Jewel into its pouch and its hiding place, Jaguar Woman then took the garnet Sin Corazón had left and prepared it for its next journey. It would be Julio who would take the bait, take the garnet in place of the Shaman's Jewel on a proposed journey for delivery at a point of ceremony. She would make sure that Sin Corazón knew that the Shaman's Jewel was to be transported. She would begin to feel the light within her, and meeting with Julio would cause a stirring inside the new openings within her heart. She knew that this would be painful for both of them at first. Just like doors that had been closed for a long, long time, their hearts would resist movement on their rusty hinges. They would fight against it and probably against each other, but eventually their hearts would open and the energy would begin to flow. Love, she hoped, would follow.

Jaguar Woman sat in her blue wooden chair next to the table, holding the garnet for a long time, rolling it around in her palm. She wanted to make sure that she was not changing the course of their emotional history through her own manipulation. That would be wrong. She wanted Sin Corazón and Julio to find themselves. She was simply making the opportunity available to them. She wanted to heal both of them. Magnificent as Julio is in the world, Jaguar Woman knew that within him, too, there were flaws that needed correction and teaching. She hoped that he would be strong enough to do so, but that was not her job as a teacher; it was José's. He was Julio's teacher, and he agreed when she had spoken with him that this was going to be a very interesting journey. She thought of Sin Corazón and her constant movement between death and life and knew that this was her last hope, but Sin Corazón herself had come to Jaguar Woman and, in her own way, had asked for help. So be it.

Jaguar Woman rolled the beautiful garnet into the medicine bag and prepared it for Julio's arrival in the morning. He would then go to San Cristóbal before going on his way to the South.

III

The bougainvillea glowed iridescent pink in the afternoon sunlight. Julio settled back in the patio chair and sipped his iced cola. He was grateful for the shade after his long, hot journey and for the feel of cold ice on his tongue. There was movement off to the left on the dining patio of the small Mexican café where he rested. It was an undulating flair, like a black chiffon scarf floating on the wind. With curiosity Julio focused his tired eyes, trying to see more clearly.

Standing in the arched adobe doorway was a woman with long black hair to her waist. She wore a long silk dress with tiny mirrors embroidered into the multicolored design of red and yellow. Almost unconsciously, Julio held a small buckskin pouch—his precious package awaiting delivery—tight against his solar plexus.

The young woman stood in silhouette against the light. Her long shapely legs cast alluring shadows under the sway of her skirt, but Julio was transfixed by the radiant beauty of her face. Her dark eyes brushed across his as she seated herself under the overhang of bougainvillea. She sat in profile to him, looking out across the mountains of San Cristóbal in southern Mexico.

Something about the shape of his neck intrigued her, the tan skin color against his white cotton shirt or the taut strength of his neck muscles, which reminded her of the smooth trunk of her sacred tree. Not surveying him directly, so as not to betray her interest, she observed Julio on the edges of her vision. He reclined in the chair, a man who obviously knew the well-honed power of his body. His movements were controlled with sure intent, but were far from being studied or self-conscious.

Suddenly Julio's laughter floated on the humidity of the afternoon. Now she turned toward him and looked at him momentarily in the eyes. A young orange cat had leapt onto his table as he fed it a scrap from his chips and salsa. She looked away, energy beginning to run up her legs and into her stomach. The cat sprang to the floor and stroked its side and back against his ankle.

Julio sighed deeply, moved his head back and forth, trying to clear his senses. What was that look in her eyes? he thought. She was beautiful, but her eyes were so dark. Was that passion he'd glimpsed? He didn't want to stare, but Julio was beside himself with fascination for this strange young woman. His heart was pounding, as if they had already spoken, as if they had already touched. Julio struggled to relax and calm his fascination for this woman. Julio was a trained *curandero* from a long history of powerful healers from the Yucatán, but never had he experienced sudden passion that threatened to overcome his better judgment and his sensibilities.

After hearing the intense hoots of an owl overhead, he finally paid attention to the warning from his spirit guardians. He listened, moved out of his trance, and watched the situation from a place of witnessing. The noise from people on the street seemed to recede as he observed the moment. An awesome glow of humidity and heat seemed to encompass the room, soft and enticing to Julio's mind, but he didn't succumb to it. Who is this woman? he wondered. She is really good. But the only response was the pounding of his own heart in his ears.

Then he realized he was still wearing his old straw cowboy hat with the flicker and parrot feathers stuck in the black leather hat band. Nodding almost imperceptibly to her, slowly he removed his hat and gently laid it upside down on the wooden chair next to him. The open-air room became still. Nothing moved, not even the radiant pink blooms on the cascading bougainvillea. Warmth and dampness encircled them, like the silence before a storm. He felt strange and struggled with a sense of obsession. Julio's unusual blue eyes flashed in spite of himself—there was no covering up the state of intrigue he found himself in. The young woman tossed her black hair and smiled, licked the edge of her tea glass, and pretended not to notice the suspense in the air.

Slowly she turned her gaze upon him. Unusual for a woman so young, her dark eyes pierced through to his soul with their power and intensity. Julio saw instantly that hers was not an innocent expression of wanting and passion. This was the look of a sorceress who embodied the eyes of death.

Julio took his hat, walked over to the woman, and bowed at the waist. "Julio Hernandez," he said, not smiling.

"Sin Corazón," she said simply.

"Come, will you walk with me? It's warm in here." Without another word they walked out onto the plaza.

Sin Corazón watched Julio like a jaguar watches its prey. Julio exchanged her predatory stare with his own. He was slightly annoyed that he could not charm her as he had the others. This one was out of reach. He couldn't decide whether to pounce upon her and fight to the death or whether to run through the fields in the moonlight, enjoying each other's power, ability, and strength.

Sin Corazón had never done a dance quite like this. Her usual tactics for seduction were not effective. She tried to invade his energy field, but she was blocked by an unseen force that annoyed her. She knew, as did he, that this could be a dance of life or a dance of death.

Julio saw her terrifying abilities, but he was not frightened by her because he had abilities of his own. He enjoyed the play of power. They lingered a long time in the soft afternoon light, looking into each other's eyes with a gaze of power that searched the depths of the other's being.

At last Julio held out his hand, open-palmed, waiting for Sin Corazón to reach out as well. Finally, she did. It was a moment when time stands still, when a magician hesitates at the center of the crossroads. The only dilemma that remains is which way to go, knowing that when you move, you move for eternity. No going back.

Sin Corazón reached out and took his hand. It was a consent unspoken, but heard loud and clear, that they were evenly matched. Echoing through the canyon walls of time, it was acceptance of equality. It was submission in the sense that she allowed him to rub up against her energy field. To Julio, it was an invitation; to her, it was an acceptance. It deeply pained Julio, knowing it was Sin Corazón who chose him. But it could be no other way. On that point they could both agree, and that evening, their dance began.

Sin Corazón did not seduce Julio, or even try. They fell in love at first sight, but didn't know it. They talked together that night. When she realized that he was carrying her own garnet and not the Shaman's Jewel, she knew that she had been tricked. But her excitement was so strong that she didn't care. They didn't realize it yet, but they both had begun to change. It was an enchanted evening.

Jaguar Woman made a sweeping gesture with her arms as we all held up our glasses of water to honor the mysterious workings of power.

"Perhaps," I said, "it will come to pass that our sister's dark soul will be illumined and their love will become vast enough to contain all the contradictions of the heart." The others laughed, and we all smiled with genuine hope.

We settled back comfortable as Jaguar Woman continued.

IV

A bright smile blazed across his deeply tanned face. His salt-and-pepper hair was thick, brushed back in dense curls to almost below his jawbone. This man was not young, but how old he was, nobody knew. When he smiled, his jagged teeth betrayed his youthful quality. His eyes twinkled at first gaze, but if you looked at him carefully, they were so deep and dark that it was as if no one lived behind them.

The old man was not happy these days, for he was losing his star pupil, his lead apprentice in the world. He needed her to do his bidding when he became tired from his work. He was very angry and full of envy for certain women in the world, and inside there was a bitter hatred for them that tasted on his tongue like burnt corn and smoke from his conjuring fire.

This particular evening he left his hut in the jungle rain forest near Belize. He walked down by the river as the sun was setting behind the dense foliage, the leaf blades on the trees shimmering emerald and shooting with rays of brilliant orange. He searched for certain roots along the banks, carefully dug them up, and put them into his sisal bag. His smile would have disarmed anyone, and his laughter was full of music and seduction. He grinned to himself as he picked the roots, knowing that a seduction was going to be part of his evening fare. He liked nothing better than to eliminate the light within another person's soul. It gave him power. It made him feel strong and healthy to do so. It gave him a reason for living.

He had never cared about goodness. He only knew within his heart that darkness and evil were stronger than people. It was his belief. He never argued for his convictions. They had never wavered from the day he was born. He had enjoyed being a dark seed for so many lifetimes, and he liked living at the bottom of the rain forest, enshrouded in decaying foliage and animal and serpent life. He dreamed only of more power to create his will, not only for himself, but within others.

The old man sat in the waning light, remembering the beautiful face of his young apprentice, Sin Corazón, and he longed for her. He longed for her, not for her body, but because he missed a kindred soul, someone who understood the depth of darkness within which he lived. When they had first met, he knew instantly when he saw the light shining in her eyes at the sight of him that she very soon could be a part of his world. He remembered sitting with her in the Temple of the Bats, the ancient ceremonial temple of his forefathers, and she had asked so many questions. He never answered questions, but on that particular occasion, he decided to entertain her curiosity. But as she was to learn, he was a sorcerer, and he never wasted his energy without a reason. As her questions formulated, he answered them with his particular dance of seduction, weaving a web of mystery and fascination around her consciousness and her heart so that she would shortly become obsessed with obtaining knowledge, what she thought was knowledge, and with the study of what she thought was personal power. Of course, it was not personal power in most of the ways of his learning. He was teaching her about darkness and the seduction of evil, but she did not know that. She had not yet learned of the hellish world in which he lived.

"What was it like?" she asked. "How did you become such a powerful sorcerer?" She sat at his feet, her beautiful eyes watching the play of light on his face. Already he could see that she adored him, and he was pleased at the reflection of his power.

"I never really knew the light," he said. "I simply was born to darkness, and I enjoyed controlling people. Don't you?"

She did not answer the question that needed no answer.

"I was a depressed child," he continued. "I looked around at my village and knew that I was in a foreign land that I did not understand. I spoke Quiché as a child, but the language seemed foreign to me. I became very remote from other children because I hated their games. I hated playing ball. I hated the silliness of their conversations. I never seemed to be young. I always was an old soul. Even my parents thought better of ever reprimanding me or trying to change me. I think they always feared me, not that they would ever admit that. There was a time as I grew older that the village was terrified of me, because they saw that I could kill any of them with just the slightest effort, and they knew that I had no heart, just like you Sin Corazón. Just like you."

"Oh, but I love people. I love the world of beauty," Sin Corazón said.

The old man laughed as he remembered the innocence flash across her lips. But then, it was soon gone. Again she was walking the edge of danger.

"I love to hear you talk," she said, "and I love your laughter. You're so wonderful," Sin Corazón said.

It was not long before she would talk often about her obsession with the old man. She was in a difficult relationship with him. He was very tough on her. He remembered hurting her often, but every time he hurt her, she came back stronger, more worthy of his teachings, he thought, always stronger, always more powerful because of the crucible of fire. He remembered refashioning her in this way through a kind of mental torture, a kind of emotional stress and pain; although horrible in its nature, it became like a drug. The pain was so dreadful when it was being inflicted, but oh, when she would recover, how beautiful she was. And he waited until again she was vulnerable and he could take her again with his treachery and seduction. What a dangerous game they had played! He even knew then that there was no winning this game, that somehow, someday, he would pay a price for the devil's dance that they had performed. But he cared not. He cared not, because he knew that behind her there was another apprentice and another and another, always someone obsessed with power, with the end justifying the means, no matter what pain to gain.

He laughed and then he frowned, because do his magic as he would, Sin Corazón seemed out of reach. What had happened? he thought. He needed to do ceremony. He needed to find her because as she had been obsessed with him, oh, he had been much more obsessed with her. He needed her vitality, and more than her vitality, he needed her womanness because he had never been able to assimilate and marry the female side of himself, and it had been the source of great weakness for him. As a result, he needed women around him, strong women; he needed her to balance him. Without her, he knew that he was in a kind of trouble that he had not suspected. He had not reckoned for this, and it was filling him with anger, but he needed the anger as well to awaken the power of his will, and he used it. He was a great and adept sorcerer who knew every trick in the trade.

So, he thought, taking out one of his stones of power from his pocket, polishing it with his thumb and forefinger, what will the dawn bring? What a fascinating world it is.

He was not fascinated with the mystery of the world, as his eyes and the expression on his face clearly showed. He was only fascinated with the dimension of his own power and the puzzle and the challenge that the warring world of darkness presented to him every day. It was always a dance of life or death, hopefully mostly death.

He was not interested in the subtleties and the harmonies of life or light. But occasionally other sorcerers before him had lost an apprentice through some form of light, and he hated that, and he wanted to destroy it with everything that was in him. He did not know why. It wasn't that light had ever betrayed him. It was simply that he needed a good enemy. He needed something to despise, to animate his intent and his life force, but he hated his enemy and wanted only to destroy that enemy. He wanted only to immerse himself in more of what he already was because for some reason, he did not care why, it sustained him. It sustained his loathsome, dark vigil on this alien planet that did not know who or what he was.

He remembered Sin Corazón asking him about his teachers.

"I have no teachers," he repeated again, "but I had my sense of loss, and I saw the pain inflicted on my people and the destruction of civilizations all around me. I lived in the ashes of lost ideals and lost hopes and dreams. Thankfully, I never needed them; I didn't need dreams. I simply lived my own dream. I have no sense of God. I saw the poor peasants taking their last centavos to the altars of a god whose face I had never seen or experienced. And I hated that god. I hated that god for our people. But then, I didn't even really care about that."

He watched Sin Corazón recoil from him when he talked about hating the church. She had always known the church as the central fire within her village.

"Let it go." He looked at her, reading her mind. "Let it go, Sin Corazón, it matters not. I will never challenge your faith, because it means nothing to me. All that matters to me is revenge."

"Revenge for what?" she asked.

"Perhaps it is revenge for being born, but unlike many of the sorcerers that I have known in the world, I take great pride and a kind of joy for the dark soul that I am. I enjoy it, and I want to share it with you."

"But you must have come from somewhere. Someone must have helped create you and your incredible abilities," she said.

"What created me was my sense of loss. Out of loss, I have created a much better world, a safer world than with those groveling peasants finding their way down an aisle of a church that does not even recognize their tradition. Oh, no, I create my own tradition. I will show you. You will understand in time."

He had looked at her at the time and seen in Sin Corazón's face that she expected to be with him only a short time, only to learn about the dark side so that she could then go back to her silly little Sisterhood of the Shields and talk about her adventures with a dark sorcerer.

How stupid, he thought. How stupid of Jaguar Woman to have been so ignorant as to have thrown this magnificent creature into his den. He would eat her, and then he would give her rebirth back into the world, transformed into a dark sorceress who would do his bidding. Had Jaguar Woman really thought that he would leave her untouched? Did she really think that he would not take her soul?

As the sun was devoured by the horizon, the old man began to prepare a mixture of herbs and other items for his ceremony. It was not a grand ceremony. No one would see this ceremony, and no one would have dreamed that he was doing it, for this old man had another life in a nearby city. He had another life, indeed, and no one would suspect it. He liked the duality of his life and the secrecy. He never asked a question because he cared not what someone else thought. He could watch someone and know their thoughts. He could observe how they functioned in the world, what they dreamed of, what their frailties and fears were. With a single statement he could elicit a reaction that would tell him everything. He was disarming.

People loved him in his everyday life. He was to them a simple man, a man of principles, a man of humor. But a strange light shown in his eyes. The people of his village would comment on the light of wisdom that they saw there, not reading and understanding that they were facing the devil himself. No one dreamed what this man could do to them. When someone crossed him, questioned him, he secretly made sure that their lives changed drastically for the worse. And no one suspected it.

It would not be long before Sin Corazón would return to him. He knew that she was with Julio and that she would tire of him. But if she didn't, then maybe he would move toward someone else close to her. Maybe he would play with Julio— yes—he liked that idea. He would get even with her. Sin Corazón would come crawling back to him.

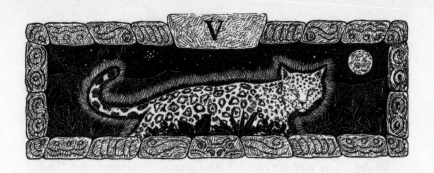

Sin Corazón had loved in her life, but those memories had all but been erased. Almost every night she tried to journey into the realms of darkness and power, looking for stimulation and revenge. But tonight was different. She couldn't look outside of herself for a diversion. So much activity was going on inside her mind and her emotions that she could not sleep, nor could she focus her intent.

Hurriedly, Sin Corazón put on her huarache sandals, a long skirt, and white cotton blouse, and burst out of the adobe hut like her feelings were bursting from her chest. She strode down the darkened path until she came to the pond filled with fish and lily pads by the plaza *mercado*.

She sat down gently on the carved stone seat by the water. If anyone had watched her from the shadows, they would have marveled at the graceful control of her body and the stealthy movements of her legs and hands. The full moon reflected silver on the stillness of the water, creating an oily soft mirror of the bougainvillea and the pine trees surrounding her. Within her yearning, Sin Corazón tried to center herself. She wondered what was happening to her. Was she becoming weak and losing her power? She was never frightened of anyone or anything, but now a shudder of unaccustomed heat rose through her body and radiated out into the dark womblike night. Suddenly, a distant voice of a woman of power pierced into her memory, and she heard Jaguar Woman's words from long ago:

"There is nothing wrong with weakness, my daughter, but only the judgment of that weakness. Weakness is a great teacher, and those aspects of yourself have brought you to your greatest heights."

Sin Corazón remembered the ensuing argument. She had admonished her teacher for allowing even the thought of weakness to enter into her consciousness. To her, weakness felt like a lack of control, as if she might fly apart into a thousand pieces if she weren't careful. And she felt that way now. Could it be that love was stalking her? The thought of Julio and the scent of his skin, the feel of his body against hers, over-whelmed her senses. Sleep brings no rest to me, she thought. It's as if a roof is caving in between its walls. Everything seems changed, altered, not as it was.

Sin Corazón leaned forward to look into the placid water's mirror. Searching for her own reflection, she saw face superim-posed upon face—the reflections of the many selves within her being. She was a woman of power who ruled her life within many domains. She ruled her domains with the exception of one—the domain of heart. She had lost her power there when her husband had left her. Now she was searching for the heal-ing. Would she have the power to take it? To her it was a game of Russian roulette—a game of life or death. Was anyone the winner? She no longer knew. The game was all that had ever mattered. She wanted that edge of pain, fear, and ultimate ecstasy. But this was a greater moment. Something new was happening, and a different bait was being presented that she knew not how to approach. She could attack, disappear, she could give away her power, or she could stand inside her cir-cle of power and experience this new feeling.

She watched the water and the moonlit clouds shifting over-head and yearned to be of the earth again. But she was a cloud. Or was she the darkness defined by the light? She searched the water for an omen, knowing she was like a fish swimming deep within the emotional ramparts of her own subconscious mind. With a fleck of light, an opening of heart would begin to expand and then shut off as quickly as it had opened. She would swim on and see pieces of bait in various forms presented before her. But her hunger was not tempted. She would not grab onto any vision, any bait. Only the light that would occasionally shine in long radiant bars through the shadows of water would interest her. Suddenly a vision came like thunder. She saw the reflection of the dark sorcerer drowning. She backed away from the pond. There was only one game left for her—the game of light and power. But not power over others, as she had experienced the Olympiad sport of life and death, but an even more mortal and yet godlike excursion into the primal wisdom of light and darkness. She knew it was her last game. This time a reckoning was upon her. She had chosen it well, before it was too late.

A gentle puff of wind blew in from a northerly direction, catching the long, curling tendrils of her hair and caressing her cheek. She sighed deeply in an effort to release the tension in her belly. She bent forward, looking to find her own reflection, but a swirling spiral of darkness, slate gray and then black, returned her gaze. She could not see herself in the mirror of water. She stared back in wonderment as the reflection took on a dimension of clear brightness and then profound emptiness, as if she were no longer there. A terror began to fill her. In some distant part of her soul she knew that a shard of her being no longer existed. It was as if she had lost her face in the pond. For a moment she wanted to search the mossy depths of the water for her lost identity, but she dared not advance or move. She felt fragile, almost beyond repair.

Her desire for Julio was burning away her resistance. Only powder was left. Soft powder like the skin on his face. She ran her fingers through the water in the same way that she had stroked his hair. It reminded her of a wild sea where danger was imminent. She became attentive and listened, with her muscles strong and ready. Sin Corazón was certain he was there guiding her hand through the water and bringing her eyes back to the transparent mirror before her. She felt his presence like a cool mist at dawn, engulfing her vision and replacing it with a mysterious blinding joy. She knew now that they were refashioning each other and that somehow he was absorbing her reflection into himself.

Like the solar eclipse of the moon, there was a dark hole in the sky and in the pond where she had seen her face. Then slowly, as if walking through a veil of sheer cognition, she began to see the outline of a face on the water that at first was unrecognizable. She wanted to run away in fear, as if a monster were trying to possess her. Then gently and with exquisite pain, tears welled up in her eyes for the first time in many years. She recognized the monster as herself and what she had become.

This was the alchemy of love. Through the gateway of prismatic light before her, spirit was returning to Sin Corazón. She experienced a sense of yielding, a sense of fire burning through her opening heart. She could not stop the progression of heat and light that was filling the horrible darkness that had been her soul. She heard a howling groan of an ancient hot wind. It was a violent upheaval of sound and emotion and transformation within her. Sin Corazón could no longer distinguish herself as being separate from Julio or anyone. The fire within her was hungry and burnt everything away.

As suddenly as the rush had started, it stopped. Once again she could sense the mist. The moon had gone behind a thunderhead, and she was surrounded in darkness. She knew he was there. She could feel him on her hands and touching her face. Sin Corazón didn't know the distance she had journeyed. But she stepped out of her eternal grief into Julio's arms. All the walking she had done, he had walked with her. Her secret pain had been like a fortress around her until now. The walls came tumbling down around them as they stood together and alone in the burst of moonlight ushering in silver and gold from behind the clouds. They stood like living jewels, their love soundlessly expressed, their secrets given to each other somewhere held between their words.

For the first time in days she slept well. But the next morning Julio was gone without a word. Her darkness had been like a drug, and Sin Corazón needed it.

VI

Sin Corazón was running now. She was crawling on the
ground, her belly close to the heart drum of Mother Earth. She
was rubbing her back against the lowest branches of the trees
to be obscure, not from loneliness but from her fear of the con-
tinuation of life. The aliveness that she had felt had somehow
wounded her, had opened her beyond her endurance, and
now she was running from her fate, from love, from hate, from
the old sorcerer, from any feeling that rose in her gut. She was
a fugitive, wandering the dimensions of the universe, like a
comet out of control, waiting to smash into something solid
that would remind her of who she was. The ground was hot
underneath her fingers. She hoped it would burn away what
was left of her identity. Why could she not die? she wondered.
What more was there left for her to do or to learn or to grasp?
When she reached out into the night air as if to grip onto some
forbidden fruit or tenuous reality, always nothing was there.
Nothingness and emptiness, but not godliness. Only pain,
coming up and bringing her down. Coming up and tearing
her apart.

She stalked through the underbrush, waiting to find a different trail away from Julio. She found no water or sustenance
or new hope, and yet new hope was the last thing she really
wanted. For a moment, in her weakness, she thought she
wanted only to be deceived and led back into the circle of
darkness. Only then would the pain abate and she would feel
alive again, and yet never again would she enter that circle. Or
would she? So there was no hope. She was too weak to love
and too wise to seek evil agin. There was no reason to survive

because this had been the last game, the only game that was left to her. Her involvement with Julio had become a game of power, and she unwittingly had joined in that game.

She sat beneath the branches of a desert willow that dropped tiny lavender orchid flowers on her shoulders and covered the ground with peace and tranquility. She sat within her tumultuous heartbreak, not understanding this fork in the trail. In the game of power she had chosen, everyone loses, for if you crush your opponent, you are left tortured with the memory of that pain. And if you are crushed, then you have lost your soul. In the game of power there is no love, only power.

Sin Corazón was a stalker, a warrioress, a woman of the dark side, and yet the light had captured her reflection and illuminated her profile in all of the heavens that surrounded her. She had been chosen once again to heal and to be brought above the tides of human emotion and endeavor. How was she to heal when nothing more survived on her inner landscape but desert and sand and the loss of foliage and nourishment? Perhaps she would wait to die now, curled up beneath the branches of the trees in the naked shadows where she had lived for so long. She knew the hidden terrain well, and yet it seemed foreign to her now. It offered no sustenance. She was a recluse within a world that had forgotten her. And she had forgotten herself. She went to sleep hoping that she would never awaken, that the torture was over, that somehow she had extricated herself in some fruitful and blessed way. She curled in upon herself, like a wolf resting her head upon her tail, and she sighed deeply into the vibrations of Mother Earth and began to breathe with the slow density of certain demise. Even the old sorcerer could not find her there.

In the morning Sin Corazón found herself by a river. She had lived within the dark abyss of her chosen nightmare for so long that a ray of light penetrating the emptiness where her heart had once existed terrified her. She thought about Julio, and something moved deep within her, a moment of creativity, a moment of expansion and radiance that she had banished from her life as weakness and impoverishment of the soul. She stood for a moment unconsciously wanting to move the power in her loins around in some way, like a pregnant mother trying to shift the baby off of a nerve within her womb. She say down again, shaking her head. She finally stopped running within herself. It had been a long time since this relationship had begun, and she had been running all this time, not only from Julio but from her own reaction. She knew that she could have destroyed him many times. But then, why hadn't she? She knew that she could have been done with the mirror that he produced for her, but she had chosen to let the mirror live.

Suddenly she grabbed a large branch from the tree standing next to her, and with her intent and her power she ripped it from the trunk. She wanted to bite the branch. She wanted to rip it into pieces. She thought of Julio and realized that something had happened that she had never wanted to happen. Perhaps now would be the time to suck the life source from his body so that she would no longer feel this torture of love. She wanted to rip his body to pieces and break his bones, tear his limbs away from his trunk like the branch in her hand. She wanted to eat him and rip his skin away with her teeth, and she wanted him always to be inside her. She wanted him to tear her to pieces, to break off her arms and rip off her head so that somehow the curse of her darkness could finally and at last leave her body.

She wanted to be a pile of sticks next to his bones so that then the Great Spirit, if the Great Spirit still existed, could refashion them. He could take a leg bone from Julio and a leg bone from her and put them together with the glue of creation, with the passion that seemed to be stalking them relentlessly day and night. She wanted to open him up and scream the eternal scream. She wanted him to listen to her and to hear everything about what she was made of. But now, she didn't know what she would say because she knew no longer who she was. She wanted him to scream his reality iinto her, to still her brain from doubt and panic and terror and bliss.

It was the bliss that was most painful to her. It was the expansion and the radiance that made her wonder if there was weakness within her now, if she had lost her power. She hated him for this and wanted to destroy him, but if she destroyed him, she would destroy herself. She took the branch in her mouth and ground her teeth into it until her gums were bloody. She wanted to taste her own blood, to sense the identity she had lost so many years ago. She wanted to feel the wind in her face blow away her pain. A strange bliss was enveloping her. The energy was coming up her spine and branching out to the millions of nerve centers, clearing her, living for a moment in her heart and then in her throat and then back down to the base of her spine, like a snake curling and warming itself in the sun, waiting to strike another day.

Sin Corazón was terrorized. She had never known a relationship where a warrior and a warrioress stood equal and yet so different. She knew that there was so much that they could not share, that there was no basis for communication in many ways, and the pain of that was on the level of personality. The female aspect of her power knew that manifestation is from the female on this earth. But what is not manifest is male. What is not manifest in the world but lives in the energy fields of the universe and the dimensions of spirit and radiance mates with the fields of manifestation and becomes evident in our lives.

For a moment she got a glimpse of what it was all about and why she had chosen the darkness for so long. She realized suddenly that the dark sorcerer had taken her into the manifestation of evil and torment, and that to be healed, she must bring in the male—the male not only in love but the male on levels unseen and as part of the great mystery. She knew that to heal she must take the reins of the great white mare of destiny that she rode. She needed to realize love, and she knew it, as her true heart began to beat for the first time in years. Sin

Corazón realized that she was in control of this blissful energy, that it was not in control of her. But she also realized that all energy and awareness has intelligence, and the energy that was filling her with bliss knew what it was doing. For her to try to control it was the play of her ego.

She remembered the words of Jaguar Woman from so long ago, those words that she had turned away from, and now she felt shame. For the first time, she realized she had turned away from oneness; she had turned away from the understanding of life and life force, from knowing that all of life has a spirit, and that you cannot separate one from the other. If there is a devil, it is someone who misses the mark, who picks the wrong target and shoots the wrong arrow, who has the idea that there is sin. If you believe there's sin, then sin is there for you, and the manifestation of sin comes from she who believes in it.

VII

Sin Corazón sat by the pond, waiting for Julio to join her. As in
the myth of Inanna, when she, unveiled, explores the darkness
of her own soul, Sin Corazón, like the fawn looking into a mirror bowl, sees not her own reflection but the image of the sorcerer Lord of the Underworld. This image sent Sin Corazón
falling back onto the carved seat, her eyes full of tears and
wonder. The monster she had seen was the dark side of Julio.
Instead of eyes of life that supported her courage for trying to
find her way out of hell, his were "eyes of death" staring
fixedly into her soul and challenging every dream of hatred
and goodness that had lived within her. She was strengthened
in the reflection and humbled. In the darkness of his eyes was
the murder of illusion. Never before had she so clearly seen
the sacred mountain within a person. But why through the
monster eyes of darkness?

Sin Corazón contemplated the moon's reflection rippling on
the water, quietly stimulated by the night breeze. A coolness
surrounded her, and she felt naked, as if even her bones were
opened and free in the night wind. Like nature, which can
only live its truth in the pure being of life, Sin Corazón dared
not survey the surface of the pond, for those "death eyes"
would scan the depths of her secret reality and find the long-
hidden truth of her emptiness. She felt the coldness of existence and nature around her like the powerful north wind at
the summit of a mountain peak.

Her fascination with challenge and power overcame her
fear. Once more she approached the depths of the pond and
wondered what gods were playing with her, torturing her in

this way. Somehow she knew the goddess within her was cracking her shell and breaking her heart into shards of light and splinters of gold. Silently she walked to the edge of the pond, afraid to look, afraid to see, afraid of the intensity of the pain. Her heart was opening like a rusty temple door that had been shut for a thousand years. As she stared into the reflection on the water, she could feel the dreamings of Julio over lifetimes. She could hear the voice of Jaguar Woman speaking of the mountains inexhaustible in their mystery and beauty. Then why the dark, demonic face of Julio, whose eyes were killing her with his limitation and uncaring coldness? Those eyes were not interested in her evil pretense or her old ways in the world. Only the jewel of her truth was being scrutinized, and she knew suddenly that her weakness would finally and at last be her salvation. Julio was entering her through her vulnerability and her powerlessness. Within her flaws was hidden the gateway that led him to her joy.

Like an oyster forming a pearl around the invading grain of sand, Sin Corazón yielded to the demonic glare that was defining her soul. The sacred mountain that she and Jaguar Woman had climbed in their teachings was inside her own flesh and was becoming part of her blood and her spirit. This was a merging, not of demons but of power, high and low and total. Sin Corazón closed her eyes and felt the mountain with its summit obscured by clouds. As she looked again into the pond, the face of Julio, kind and full of love, looked back at her. His eyes had changed again into goddess eyes, the eyes of life. The fires of the spirit of place were rekindled in her heart, and she burned with joy.

Sin Corazón looked up to find Julio looking at her intently. She watched his eyes as they perused her face and her body. Again she felt the mountain inside him, the immensity of his sacred landscape. Could she find her way through this wilderness plain? Was there food for her spirit, or would she die of hunger? Somehow, one question would lead to another in her mind until she came to no questions and only the possibility of overwhelming danger.

"What happens when one dangerous person meets another dangerous person?" she asked.

"Then there is danger times two, like a double black diamond. This is more dangerous than heading for a cliff, this game we are playing," he said, tearing her heart out with his indecision. "Do you think you could be happy with me?"

"Yes," she answered. "What are you afraid of?"

"Expectation about time mostly, and other things, too, but mostly how our separate needs would impose on each other's freedom."

Julio sucked his energy back away from her then, and as he did so, Sin Corazón's energy surged out to him, involuntarily, like a tidal wave filling a sea cave. Julio stood over her in a trance state, healing her body with his intent, and she watched in awe as he died before her eyes. Then with a jerk of his limbs, he returned to life, and her own energy plunged back into her body in an undulating wave of sexual stimulation.

She had no control over what was happening. Sin Corazón had been emptied and then refilled with her own power. She watched him carefully as he talked and played with her. He was irresistible in his repertoire. An errant thought crossed her mind as she moved back into her own circle of power. Sin Corazón was feeding him her power with every word she spoke, every gesture, with every caress. And that was her invitation for him to die into her. Only then would they have the mysterious power it takes to die into each other. He in turn was filling her with power and tiny trancelike deaths. She experienced the life of him, and then the death of him, only to see him be reborn, as her energy enabled him to fly.

"Man is given power by woman. He is impregnated by her." She heard the voice of Agnes Whistling Elk.

Without Sin Corazón's love for Julio, the nurturing garden could not have been prepared. Without Julio's love, the garden

could not have been planted. Without the combined force of
their depths of love, the alchemy of creation could not have
been born. Out of the forest, the goddess of returning love
came with stars swimming in her hair and in the trees around
them. Sin Corazón clenched her fingers and opened her arms,
as if to hold on to this moment of completion forever.

11
Invitation from the Dark Side

For the next few days we took a break from the story of Sin Corazón and Julio. Agnes and I went to a neighboring village to stay with Zoila, who was visiting her husband's family. Zoila stays there often, I learned, when she is doing ceremony with Jaguar Woman.

Agnes and I were both exhausted emotionally from the story and all that had transpired. I wrote for long hours, sitting out in the cornfields behind the wattle-and-daub house. Agnes, in turn, would disappear into the wilderness for hours and return with fragrant herbs to take back to Canada.

Ruby had stayed with Jaguar Woman. I dared not ask what they were doing. I was sure I would be informed soon enough.

I sat in a small restaurant off the plaza *mercado*. The red awnings flapped in the hot, summer wind that had come up from the south about half an hour before. It was a humid day, and I felt exhaustion and extreme trepidation as I sipped an iced tea and looked into the eyes of the sister-woman Sin Corazón, who was across from me. It had been a long time since I had seen her in that ceremony of banishment in the Yucatán.

I had been awakened early in the morning a week ago in my hut outside of Uxmal in the Yucatán. Zoila had handed me a letter mailed from Mérida and then left me alone with it. I had no idea what the letter contained, but I sensed in Zoila's gaze that it was of importance. The letter had been from Sin Corazón and was an invitation to meet her in San Cristóbal a week hence.

Stunned, I took the letter directly out under the ceiba trees in front of Zoila's house. Her hair was pulled back at the nape of her neck. She wore a thin white cotton blouse embroidered with brightly colored threads, a long blue skirt, and huaraches. The strength of her body was noticeable as she knelt on the ground with grace and carefully picked her herbs and dug in the earth with a small spade.

"Zoila, you knew this was from Sin Corazón, didn't you?" She nodded.

"She wants me to meet with her. Does that seem right?" I asked, helping Zoila to gather the plants.

"It's appropriate only if you wish to do so."

"Will there be harm in this?" I asked. "And what would she want with me?"

"What do you think?" Zoila asked.

She finally stopped digging and sat on the ground. She patted the ground next to her for me to sit.

"Sometimes," she said, "there is a wildness inside of us that is like a room full of beasts. It's a terror for most of us to ever open a window or a door and let those beasts out. You think it's a room full of tigers waiting to devour you. If you have a sense of responsibility, you know that it is very dangerous to open that door and let that wildness out because you don't know what form it may take. And once they're out, who knows if you can control them?"

I looked at her in amazement and then understood that she was describing not only Sin Corazón, but an aspect of all of us.

"But Zoila," I said, "isn't it true that some of us know that wildness in a different way? Not only as wildness, but as a darkness as well?"

"Yes." Zoila nodded, holding up her herbs as she tied them in bundles. "You see, if you repress your natural instincts, whatever they may be, they create a shadow self. It's part of your shadow shield, the darkness. How that instinctual nature is suppressed and what you have allowed yourself to do in ceremony to heal it depend on many things, such as on your history, your spirit history."

"With Sin Corazón, however," I said, "there was a great fascination for black magic and sorcery."

"There is no question," Zoila said. "That is where she has lived for a long time."

"But I felt, Zoila, during the banishment ceremony that Sin Corazón will move through this and come out on the other side a healed person, or at least with the possibility of transforming. Do you think that's true?"

Zoila, who had been much closer to Sin Corazón than most of us, shook her head. "I wish that I did know what to say to that, my daughter. Sin Corazón may have come to a place where she needs a friend, and if you can be strong enough not to be taken in by anything that she may say or do, then going to see her could be a good thing.

"That's a decision only you can make. You know your own power. There's no way that you, of all people, could be swayed by someone like her. Of all the apprentices I have ever known, you have an innocence that simply has never left you. That innocence has allowed you to learn far beyond the borders of consciousness than you ever imagined. But on the other hand, it can be your downfall with someone like Sin Corazón because you may not be able to see her properly. So it might be very interesting to be a fly on the wall at that meeting. Sin Corazón is not of an innocent heart, but maybe one day she can become pure of heart. That remains to be seen. My fear for you, my daughter, would be that you would not see her trickster self coming, if she chose to use it."

"I would see it," I said a bit emphatically.

Zoila smiled at me. "Perhaps we could do ceremony and make sure that your dreambody is very strong before you go. If you are prepared, if you understand what you are meeting, then I think that you will see her very well. But in your innocence, do not think that you can heal her. You can only love her. Sin Corazón must transform herself." Zoila paused as she pinched dead leaves off a stem of cilantro. "But I think that she may have had a little help."

"You mean Julio?" I asked, catching the glint in her eye.

"Well," Zoila said, "it is possible that love may have touched her."

"They seem to be doing quite a dance together," I said.

"Because of what has happened, I think Sin Corazón needs a friend. You are the youngest among us. She will feel closer to you than to anyone. I think I will send you with my blessing. Jaguar Woman is gone right now, but we will dream with her tonight and make sure that we are of a similar mind. Sin Corazón is a sister, even though she has fallen away. We have loved her and we will always love her. Maybe she has learned how to call back those wild spirits that were in her. Maybe she has learned that in giving up control, she has gained it totally."

That night Agnes, Ruby, Zoila, and I went to the ruins of Uxmal to do ceremony. The great Mayan Temple of the Magicians stood in stony repose against the silver shield of the moon. The night birds of the jungle joined us in song.

"Never fight a powerful force, even if you could overcome it. Never clash directly with power. You might break something," Zoila said to me as we circled the fire in ceremony, dancing and walking as we talked.

"If you move in a circle—her power comes from in front of or in back—she's defenseless from the side, no strength," Agnes said, poking my side. "Like swimming in a rapids, edge your way over to the shore from an angle. Make an arc to get at an angle to her. Go with the current and deflect her a little with each act of aggression. Each act of aggression violates a law of energy."

"Remember that," Ruby said, poking me from the other side. "If you go with the force, it will take you to safety. A hurricane will blow itself out; a tidal wave will wash you ashore.

The energy required to produce the force is finite and will end at some point."

"Nothing in nature that has mass has that much energy," Agnes said from the other side of me as we circled. "It will expend itself. Once expended, that is the moment of vulnerability."

"Don't back or move in a straight line," Zoila said as the women spun me around. "You move out of harm's way in a circle. No human is powerful enough to put energy out in all four directions at once. If you retreat, do not retreat in a straight line. If you do, Sin Corazón will always know where you are."

"Don't pull your swing or your hips," Ruby said, patting her red baseball hat with her flattened palm. I stopped in surprise at the slang and redirection of energy by Ruby into playful Americana.

"Hey," I said, smoothing my sides. "I've got great hips!"

We all laughed and the suspense was broken. The moment in ceremony deepened even more.

"Why have you asked me to meet with you, Sin Corazón?" Sin Corazón was a most extraordinary woman. Her beauty was awesome, her hair sleek and black, her eyes flashing, watching. I always had the feeling that she missed nothing and saw things that others never saw.

I looked carefully into her eyes, searching for the darkness that I knew had been living within her soul. "Have I changed that much?" Sin Corazón asked, sitting back in her chair. She was dressed simply in a shorter dress from the region of Mérida. Her earrings were silver and glinted, reflecting the light of the sun. Her skin was deeply tan, and a turquoise Navajo necklace hung around her neck. She obviously was a woman of power.

We looked at each other for a long time. It was as if we were two cats circling a mouse that happened to be the iced tea and the chips and salsa on our table. Perhaps we were both looking for an entrance, a gateway, a way of communicating, a way of understanding each other without harm. At least I could say that for me. But for her, this was something I needed to discover.

It was just as Zoila had suspected: "Because I need a friend," Sin Corazón said. "I have been through so much since we have left one another. I thought I would never see any of you again, and if I did it would only be in a situation of contention where we would be vying for power. But I am not here to confront you, Lynn. I am here because we were friends. There is no way that you could not forgive me, because that is your nature. But no matter what harm people have done you, as I have seen many times in our friendship together over the years long ago, your forgiveness was profound. I guess," she said, looking down for the first time and looking almost shy, as if she did not want me to see tears welling in her eyes, "I have lost my way for a very long time, and I am trying to find my way home."

She looked at me now, her face quite different. As with all women and men of power whom I have ever known, when their power shifts, their physical being and stature shifts visibly. Right now she looked much younger. I could have sworn there were fewer lines in her face than had been there just moments before. She folded her hands in her lap and looked at me from a place of pure heart—or so it appeared.

"I am sorry for the confusion and the pain I have caused you, Lynn," she said in a tiny voice. "I know that I hurt you deeply when I chose a different way. Something in me needed to be released, and I could go no further on my path of life without understanding the demons that swept me away into the darkest corners of the night. I needed to love them, and in setting them free, at least I would have control over them by the choice that I had made, because they were beginning to control me."

"But they did control you, Sin Corazón, and they took you from us."

"No, Lynn, I took myself from you, and I know that now. I have no one else to blame but me. If there is darkness in this world, we choose it, and we must be responsible for what we are."

"And who are you now, Sin Corazón? Because for all of the experiences we've had together in our lives, I don't know you anymore."

"Then simply experience me, Lynn, as I sit here, and when I feel the love from you that is you, I can only heal. In the mirror that you create for me, I know that perhaps there is hope, even for someone like me."

I looked at Sin Corazón for a long time, watching the lights around her. No matter what fun, what learning, what journeys we took together, I never remembered Sin Corazón with such openness of heart. She had always been closed or semi-closed, with a coolness about her that now seemed to be gone.

"What has happened to you to open your heart so?" I finally asked. "You really are truly changed in some way. Certainly it cannot be the dark path of sorcery—"

She interrupted me. "No, certainly not that in any way. I met someone, and someone has changed me."

"Someone has changed you?" I asked.

"A decision was made between us, a decision for growth, a decision for transformation, and somehow he absorbed into his own power the reflection of my darkness. At first I thought this man might be interested in the sorcery that I was trying so hard to leave behind me. But I'm assured now that he is help-ing to heal me."

"But how can that possibly be, Sin Corazón? You and I both know that you can only heal yourself. No one heals you."

"No, no one heals you. I often thought that," Sin Corazón said. "But somehow there is a way energetically to merge with another human being in the process of love. And when that merging happens, rare as it may be, it is indeed possible to end the long midnight search for sorcery and manipulation. Maybe in this lifetime or in other lifetimes, it finally happens, and you come face-to-face with a reflection, sometimes literally, in the waters of the universe, and when you see yourself, you see a monster. You can fall in love with that monster and make it even bigger, or you can transform that monster and become goodness again. When I saw that monster as myself, it was as if my flesh were falling away, as if I could not breathe, as if there would be nothing left of me, nor did I care," she said. "But slowly, through love, slowly through illumination, I merged with his radiance and somehow had the strength to overcome the demons that had overtaken me."

"Are you saying that you were a victim of these demons?" I asked, taking a long sip of my iced tea and watching Sin Corazón move back into a younger-looking woman before my eyes, the lines again disappearing around her eyes.

"Yes, I am saying that I was victimized by my own creation, but somehow in the creation of that monstrous painting, I got lost in the landscape of it and couldn't find my own way out. Sometimes when you look at the darkness too long, the darkness begins looking at you. Then the darkness takes you. Whatever that means, Lynn, I am now out of the labyrinth, lonely, and yet full. I know myself completely now. And now I have to find a process of redemption. It helps me to see you, to talk to you, to hear my own voice, and to see the Sisterhood reflected in your eyes because I have missed you so. Thank you for meeting with me. It means everything to me."

Sin Corazón reached out and set a tiny fetish of a black wolf in front of me. She held her fist to her heart, and she nodded her head to me in respect.

"To my sister spirit," she said as she left, "if she will remember me."

Sin Corazón turned and like leaves on the wind was gone so quickly that I wondered for a moment if she had actually even been there.

VIII

Agnes, Ruby, and I had rejoined Jaguar Woman for the story-telling. The story was becoming a part of me. I saw aspects of myself in both Julio and Sin Corazón, aspects of my own concerns in relationships.

Julio was walking toward the mountains. They were not far. He needed to retreat to the highest point of land around. There was an opening, a chasm, within his own being that needed tending to. Was this a new canyon for water to flood? The floodgates of emotion that he was holding back seemed relentlessly to be pushing against the gates that held them, but he could not identify those gates. He could not imagine why he was using so much energy to resist this beautiful woman, but resisting he was. He knew that she felt this. For a moment he wanted to run to someone else. In another moment he wanted never to feel these feelings again because the possibility of light and intensity and strength and humor tortured him, because it felt like weakness. He realized that what he was feeling was most likely what she was feeling, and that terrorized him too because as he was running, he knew that she was running. As a *curandero*, as a man of power, he had helped heal Sin Corazón, and he knew it. He knew that night at the pond he had absorbed her darkness into himself, and somehow through the magic and the alchemy of power he had transformed those dark aspects of her into a new beginning, into light, into a process of becoming, and he was a part of that becoming. He knew it with every cell of his being, but he did not know the form. He knew as a *curandero* that to do his magic, to heal, to be a man of power, he must have form.

In his work with José he had been taught many keys, many sacred wheels of truth, aspects of power. He knew well how to heal, how to work with the forces of nature, the allies that move across the deserts and jungles of Mexico like a curling mist of heat. But this was a new experience for him. He thought that he had explored the realms of love, of physical relationships with women, but never had he met a woman like Sin Corazón who stood equally with him. Where he surpassed her, she at the next turn would surpass him. He knew no form for this. He had a picture in his mind of the beatuy of expression between himself and Sin Corazón, but he had no frame of reference to enclose this work of art. As a result, the reality of his relationship with her was fringing off into different parts of his life where, perhaps, they did not belong. He had been comfortable while in the process of healing Sin Corazón, while in the process of healing himself as well, because there is always an exchange of energy within the process of moving toward evolvement. But now he, too, was in a place of stillness, but his stillness was different from hers. His stillness was in a place of not knowing. He knew that the next move had to be his, and he seemed unable to advance, to reach out. As Sin Corazón was unable to make a move, his position was similar but different because he knew, as did she, that it was up to him. If the magic was to work for them, he had to begin the next spiral dance.

He searched the horizons of his mind, the great quaking trees of his experience, as he moved toward the mountain, the top of the mountain, the pinnacle that was his position of reflection, a place where ideas always came to him, where he sorted out what no longer served him. He was tired as he trekked toward the summit. His legs ached, the muscles ached in his back, and he stressed and strained, unaccustomed to the depth of tiredness that he was feeling. His heart quickened, not from the effort in his physical body but from anxiety, with a sense of unsureness that infuriated him. And in his anger, his strength returned, and he leapt toward the summit, his destination of hopeful peace.

As he sat finally on his ledge at the summit and looked out toward the setting sun, the western gateway that always filled him, he felt a strange excitement instead. He looked deep within himself. In his *curandero* ability to see, he moved down into the energy of things that circulated around his place of power in his belly. He moved with the flow of energy, and he let go of his ideas and his yearnings. At last the stillness came. At last a moment of release surrounded him and filled him with a golden light, not unlike the sun that was slipping behind the horizon and out of sight. And now as darkness fell, he moved into those shadow places within his own being and forced himself to look at aspects of his own power and reckoning that he had never faced before. He asked himself about his own sense of power. Did he feel that somehow he did not deserve to be happy? With a surge of emotion he realized that in fact this might be true, that perhaps there was a part of himself that really was afraid, for the first time, to be hurt, to be deceived, afraid to die in some way. As the sun died behind the horizon, he knew also that in the morning there would be a morning star to guide the sun on its way back toward its zenith in the sky, to its place of power and growth and life-giving energy. He, too, would follow that morning star, that Venus in disguise, which if we are lucky enters and lives within the hearts of us all.

IX

Sin Corazón walked down to the edge of the sea. She looked out across the vast expanse of blue water, rolling in soft ground swells from the horizon. She sat down on the sand, looking out at a wharf that sliced its way into the lagoon. She imagined herself standing at the end of that wharf, her face turned into the wind. She imagined a storm, wild and tumultuous, raging around her, tearing at her clothes, pelting her with rain, washing her free from her emotions and thoughts, the travail that led her to the end of the dock. She saw herself looking deep down into the depths of the sea. Then Sin Corazón imagined the eye of the storm and that she was standing at the center. The storm raged about her, a hurricane miles away far offshore, coming to pelt the edges of the sea and the land with sheeting fragments of water and foam. She imagined what it would be like to stand there untouched by the power and force of the winds and sea, and she felt completely absolved from previous pain and yearnings. Somehow she was untouched, unscathed by the powerful waves of wind that rocked the ocean around her, and as the wind swirled in a spiraling movement, the waves, now six, now eight, even ten feet high, great long tunnels of white foaming surf, rolled in and crashed on the sandy beaches. But tethered to the dock, unswayed by the surging power of nature around her, she stood in a place of stillness, a place of silence, and for the first time Sin Corazón listened to her own wisdom.

Then off in the distance she heard the voice of Jaguar Woman telling her, as it had so very long ago, that there was still time, that with her power and her remembrance of who she was, her original nature, that this evil dream spell could be broken. At first, Sin Corazón knew not what the voice meant. Did she mean the spell of love? Did she mean the darkness that she had chosen in the depths of the jungle when her husband had left her? It was then that Sin Corazón realized that whether her husband had left or not, she had always had a fascination for the magical dark side, that there had been a time when even though she was influenced by the power and the brilliance of Jaguar Woman, her secret wanderings in the night were always to the citadels of evil. She knew, finally, that evil lies in the hearts of men and women who manipulate and misuse their power for their own jealousy and greed and revenge. Her path had been a path of revenge. She had tried over and over again to revenge herself against her husband and against the woman who had taken him, and then she realized that no good marriage can ever be broken. A strong, conscious marriage can be shaken but never destroyed. She had lost her awareness of her husband. There was no blame. How could she have been so blind, she wondered, still sensing the tumultuous seas around her. She saw within herself the storm, a tsunami of wave and draw and reaction to the powerful elements that emblazoned her being. Sin Corazón had caused the storm. Sin Corazón in her power had called up her ally winds of destruction, and she had enjoyed every minute of it, but that brief distraction had robbed her. Those moments of sweet revenge had robbed her of her soul.

If only Jaguar Woman were here, she thought. She would know the answer to the question that burns in my mind. If I have lost my spirit, where is it now?

She knew that she must go to Jaguar Woman, that she must see her teacher once again. She knew that for all that she had become, Jaguar Woman had turned away from her, taken her power away from Sin Corazón. Would she consider a meeting? she wondered.

Sin Corazón sat down inside her own deepest consciousness, and she pulled up the image of the Temple of the Sun.

Within that temple, she saw the secret doorway that led into the inner chamber. The inner chamber was of ancient Olmec design, a temple forgotten beneath the earth, covered with vines. This temple was a ceremonial structure and was little known to the outside world. It had been a seat of power for the women in the Sisterhood for centuries, since the beginning of their work together on this continent. Sin Corazón knew the entrance, she knew the password, and she paid respect and homage to the guardian jaguars at the door.

In Sin Corazón's deep trance a black panther circled her four times, sniffing at her, looking into her eyes to see if they were true, and finally licking her hand with a long pink tongue, it led her way into the center of the temple in Sin Corazón's mind. As if she were really there, Sin Corazón could smell the ancient, damp quality of the earth beneath her feet, the carefully hewn stones that had been cut to fit so many centuries ago.

She called out the power song for Jaguar Woman, but the sacred seat of forgetting and remembering sat empty in the tomb of the highest goddess that reigned there. She knelt before the Jaguar Seat, and as is customary, she remembered all of whom she was. She cried from the depths of her being, remembering the many forks in the trail and the wrong turns that had been made, the turns into darkness, the trails that led beneath the trees, avoiding the light, always hidden in the mystery of the unknown.

Then she looked into the lodge of forgetting. She burst through those memory banks, like a great galleon at sea, bursting through the waves, frothy waves of white water, glistening in the sun. She could see the water; she could smell the earth; she felt the stones beneath her feet. She could still see the storm circling her at the end of the wharf, and yet at the same time she found herself within the old Mayan Temple of the Jaguar. She let go of what had held her for these many years. She let go of the claws of darkness that had sunk themselves deep into her power center. She extracted the curling claws of the old sorcerer and bled into the sacrificial bowl that had been placed at her feet. She forgot herself to herself and remembered herself to herself. As one returns, one longs to go home, and her yearning blazed her trail through her own forest of weakness and jeopardy.

She called out for Jaguar Woman to come to her, to help her, as never before, for Sin Corazón had never asked for help; she had never felt the need. She had never been down a trail that she didn't understand until now. Then a familiar voice, a female voice of power, began to speak from the corners of the chamber. Sin Corazón dared not look toward the voice because she knew that Jaguar Woman would be standing there, piercing her ignorance with her shining eyes.

"It is love that has brought you to me once again, and it is out of love that I stand before you once again. I see your pain, and I see that you are a woman who tries to pull the pieces of her soul back together into wholeness. I see the trail that you have lived. I will not punish you, for that is not my place within your life. Your existence has been punishment enough. It has been punishment enough for anyone to have survived. So, Sin Corazón, what is it that you want of me? Let your intent be known to me, now."

Sin Corazón was painfully aware that Jaguar Woman would not take her seat of power. It meant that she was unsure of their position together. She stood on the periphery of Sin Corazón's life, watching her, praying for her, and abandoning her to her choices and dark dreams.

"I long for completion," Sin Corazón said to the voice in the shadows. "If that means death, then I am ready to die. If it means love, please help me and point my way down this unfamiliar trail. I don't know that I can bear it any longer. What is to become of me?"

In the vision Sin Corazón knelt before the Jaguar Seat. She felt the depths of her vulnerability. Finally, she turned toward Jaguar Woman, the woman who had been her teacher. Jaguar Woman, under the steadiness of her gaze, walked out from the shadows, her power so extraordinary, her being so radiant, that Sin Corazón blinked away the tears in awe at the remembrance of who her teacher really was.

"It is not for me," Sin Corazón said, "to ask forgiveness, for my extraordinary ignorance is so profound I know not even where to begin. Look into my heart, my teacher; look into where the essence of my being lives and see me. If I come to you out of lies and deception, then kill me now, for I have lost my way. And if I am so ignorant of myself, then perhaps I no longer deserve to live."

Jaguar Woman circled her errant apprentice four times. She used the celestial rattle that had been sacred in their teachings together. Sin Corazón was drawn back into the circle of power with every shake of the rattle. The soft crystals against the ancient gourd brought tears to her eyes and wisdom into the presence of the two women even as they stood in a dream.

"I see a woman," Jaguar Woman said, finally taking her place on a chair, sitting with the graceful posture of a young girl. She was powerful and kind as she sat in her brilliant dreambody before Sin Corazón . "I see a woman, nothing more and nothing less. I see a woman who had the courage to live her fascination. I see a woman who followed the darkness of her dreams to no good end. You have paid dearly for what you didn't understand, as do we all." Jaguar Woman touched her fist to her heart, and the tears in her eyes echoed well the depths of emotion that Sin Corazón was feeling.

Sin Corazón had forgotten the tumultuous sea and the storm and the wharf and the sand. It was as if she were sitting inside the Temple of the Jaguar. She wondered at the clearness of the vision around her. She did not care how it was happening. All that mattered was that she was feeling reunited with her teacher.

"I do not judge you," Jaguar Woman continued. "I only love you, and beyond anything that you can imagine, I am relieved that you are here. Julio is a great *curandero*. In his love for you, he has absorbed your dark reflection, if you will remember."

Sin Corazón gasped, remembering that night as she had searched the mirrorlike surface of the water for her own reflection and had found none. She had suspected it then, but in her terror she had run away from Julio and her fate, whatever that may be. "But I—"

Jaguar Woman continued, interrupting her. "He has helped you to reform yourself. There was no other way. But you, you are the one," she said, pointing to her, "who created the merging. It is from your power that your rebirth has occurred. Julio was there for you. Julio loves you, and you him. Through the power of love you discovered that the only way darkness could be abated was through love. You found your way to that healing threshold before it was too late. Now it is up to you. He has done his magic. He has brought you to you. When you look into the pond now, you see not only your own reflection but also the reflection of the eyes of life that support you and give you strength. May you join those eyes with your own and become one with all that is."

Sin Corazón looked into her face, the face of this teacher whom she loved so much. "I have been gone a very long time, many, many lifetimes," Sin Corazón said, "and it is as if I only left yesterday, but my heart is filled with terror at the thought of this marriage, because we, Julio and I, are dangerous people."

"But you are not dangerous to each other in love. Only in that love will you transform," Jaguar Woman said. "So I say to you, 'I set you free.' When you have completed the circle with Julio, we will meet again, and know that my love is with you as well, and my blessings, for you have done well. You have found the hidden trails that have led you back home. Rebuild your lodges and live within your own circle of power. Only then can our work together begin again. In every ending is a beginning, and in every beginning is an ending. All of life is a circle."

After her meeting with Jaguar Woman in the Temple of the Jaguar, Sin Corazón, still sitting on the beach, thought to herself in wonderment, considering for a moment if her meeting had been real. Then she knew beyond doubt that the energy of Jaguar Woman's dreambody had been with her, and there truly had been an exchange of power and healing medicine.

Sin Corazón felt a quietude not only surrounding her but in her, as if she had moved to a new and unfamiliar plateau. No wonder she had imagined the storm because, indeed, she felt as if she lived at the center of a tumultuous gale of wind and storm and force. There was a stillness inside her, no need to move, to reach out, or to retreat. She simply sat within a new sense of wisdom and something that she knew as a kind of bliss, a settling of a kind, but she did not know what she was settling for. She knew that many demons had been slain, demons that had accosted her, tempted her, many of whom she had followed unwittingly into the dark lodges of the universe. Now she sat within her own self-lodge, exploring for the first time in many years the dusty walls, the *nichos* standing open with no sacred icons. She wandered down lonely passageways within the temples of her heart and spirit. She searched for Julio, for his energy, for that place of sweetness, and yet danger lurked there around them. She and Julio seemed caught in an eternal dance of light and shadow. She now was still, waiting, wondering, and yet, magically, expecting nothing.

When Sin Corazón thought of Julio, she wanted to run, but something arrested her movement and kept her still even though she wanted to flee. When she analyzed the strength of the mystery that surrounded her, she realized that it came from a certain aspect of Julio that was the killer, the part of him that was made of steel, that was impenetrable, that knew what was right and wrong, what was important and could never be changed. It was that aspect of him that kept her moving and yet still within her own consciousness. It was that aspect of him that she knew could destroy her if he should decide to turn on her. Within Julio it was that aspect of her that could destroy him, that kept him from moving toward her and taking her completely.

She realized that there was a dilemma. She knew not what to do, except movement was indicated now. So she moved off the beach, away from the sea and the symbol of the Jaguar Temple but never again away from the beckoning love of her teacher. She moved toward the desert, away from the jungles, away from the places of sorcery that had seduced her for so long. She moved toward the essence of water, of emotional liquidity, of waves, but not waves of up and down, of torture and joy and more torture. She moved toward the desert that had at one time been the bottom of the sea but was now the forgotten essence of the sea. And she waited, not in stillness, but in movement. As she moved she created, and as she created, a seduction of joy and goodness began to grow within her heart.

Julio looked out across the vast expanse of desert from his high plateau on the mountain. He watched a condor circling in the high air drafts, looking for prey far below. Julio stretched out his arms and stood and did the dance of the condor that he had learned from José in the ceremonies for the solstice. He circled the plateau, dipping, stretching his wings. He closed his eyes, deep in a trance, feeling the air drafts lifting him above the ground. After a long time of silent dance in and out of the shifts in the wind, his body began to levitate a few inches, hovering above the ground in silent ceremony. His intent was so power-ful and strong that no other thought entered in, not his love, not his confusion, only the spirit of his god.

When he came back to light upon the ground, he sat down again on his heels, his knees bent as he looked out toward where the sun had emblazoned the horizon. He thought to himself about the condor and the birds of prey that he loved so much, the hawks that lived within his heart. He thought that what deepened him most in life was a sense of freedom, free-dom to practice his art, freedom to heal, freedom to be himself at every turn, like the condor high in flight above him. The condor knew no restriction in space or time, only the instinct in his belly of hunger and fulfillment. His instincts made him part of the magical universe that surrounded him. Julio, too, wanted to be free, to be able to float always on those currents of magic and power without restriction. Then he closed his wings, settled his arms down around him, and he put his palms flat on the earth, feeling the power of the mountain surging up into his arms and into his shoulders.

How could he live with a woman, ever? Commitment to him had always meant a loss of freedom. He heard José's voice quiet in the distance of his mind. He remembered a conversation he had had once with José and Zoila, who were married not only in the physical realm, but in spirit. José had said to Zoila that in losing his freedom he had gained it, totally and completely, forever. Julio thought for a long time about those words because to him any kind of commitment to any human being other than his teacher was a loss of independence and something that meant a kind of death to him. There was a similarity to him in the process of always becoming in his life. He wanted that process of becoming, but to end that becoming, to arrive finally at his destination, meant a kind of death in the process of life, as did marriage.

Julio stood on his plateau, his mountaintop, looking across the summit, the peaks of his life, wondering if he should jump from peak to peak like a billy goat, mostly in the air, touching the earth seldom and only very gently. Was that the kind of commitment he would have to make—gently touching Sin Corazónin and then leaving her forever to her own devices? Somehow he knew that there had to be more for her and more for him.

He thought again of José and Zoila, who worked their magic in the world very differently, who lived in all of the dimensions of the universe and yet were not restricted by those dimensions in any way. Buy they were not formless people either. José had often accused Julio of being too formless, that at some point he had to draw a frame around the magnificent picture of his life, to enhance it, to give it power and definition. Julio did not know if he could learn that lesson in this lifetime. He now felt like leaping off this mountain, sliding down the mountain at breakneck speed, tempting the forces of death and life to approach him so that the dilemma of love would no longer touch him. Perhaps he would be free this time, free at last forever, floating with the clouds in the midnight sky.

As the ravens quietly winged their way overhead on the slow, relentless wind, Sin Corazón circled and landed silently within the security of her own consciousness. She listened to the water flow in a nearby fountain. As dawn colored the horizon with an orange glow, she began to recover her senses out of the torpid wanderings through her nightmarish ecstasy and sleep. What has happened? Her thoughts wandered through what she had seen that night. Sin Corazón felt annihilated, tortured, and transformed. Now she slowly moved into a blissful state of floating like the clouds above her. She watched them billowing above her as she lay down on the grass near the pond. Feeling the surge of energy from Mother Earth healing her, she allowed her heart to beat in cadence with the heart pulse of nature. She realized that her past weaknesses and obsession with power were gone, and she was losing her relationship with the negative forces that she had known all these years as the central controlling instinct in her life. Now she did not know what would happen. She had always wanted control. Now she was out of control. If Julio came to her it would be part of nature. He would come with the ebb and flow of the tides and the essence of the gravity of things. Sin Corazón had let go. Perhaps it was her effort to bring him near that had kept him away. Or perhaps there was nothing holding him near, and he would fly away from her. Total freedom had encompassed her like a cocoon giving birth to a butterfly, and there was no dilemma and no pain left, only the light that she sensed glowing inside her that could never again be stolen.

Collector of Death

Something was wrong. The old sorcerer could not find his apprentice. He had been doing ceremony through the night and into the day. He was angry.

"How stupid of Sin Corazón to think that she could leave me ever," the old sorcerer muttered, stabbing his special knife into a tree stump. He looked up into the sky to watch the turkey buzzards circling in a figure eight in the sky above him. For the first time in his life, his heart sank with a feeling of fear, not fear of revenge or imminent danger, but fear that perhaps he was getting old, that he was, perhaps, losing his power. He placed his hands flat on the ground. He closed his eyes, and he felt the energy of the Temple of the Sun moving up into his body. This renewed him and abated his rush of fear for a moment. As he felt that energy he also realized that in some way he had been challenged. Was it Jaguar Woman, was it Sin Corazón herself, or was it simply life challenging him beyond his depth, beyond perhaps even his vast limits of what he knew in the world of magic? Then a flash of light in front of the old man blinded him momentarily.

With the intensity of his thoughts he had not noticed the storm clouds overhead. A blast of west wind hit him in the face, and a lavender-and-gold shard of lightning crackled through the jungle with immense clarity and force. Like a lightning rod, an antenna for the harbingers of death and destruction, the sorcerer's knife was illuminated with the electrical charge and melted before the sorcerer's eyes. The knife had been his wand of power. The sign of mystery was unmistakable.

Stunned by the lightning and the event, he sat in the awesome glow of the burning tree stump for a long time until the fire was only smoldering coals, diminishing hope of light in the jungle darkness. He knew for sure that Sin Corazón was gone in the way that he had known her and that he would leave her alone for a while. He would try to replace her. To him she was dead as she had been, and he would do ceremony, now, as if one of his own children had passed on to the other side. He did not know how, exactly, his fate had come to this because ordinarily he would never give up a chase.

It would only spur him on to new and more strenuous ceremony, but something inside him told him that their old way of working was finished. His great knife was gone. Perhaps he had done what he needed to do with her, and she had given him what she could. Now the bonds were broken.

As he made that decision, the collector of death above him flew away to the west, and he knew that sign well. He knew it as a sign of completion. As the sun rose in intensity and heat, bringing a new day, he swept his crystals into his bag and prepared for an all-day and all-night ceremony of death and ritual and rebirth, because now he must find a new apprentice. But he was still not through with Sin Corazón or Julio. His relationship with Sin Corazón had simply changed. It was up to him to redefine their relationship.

XIV

Julio and Sin Corazón walked along a trail deep in the wilderness of Chiapas. A stream meandered next to them as they walked, and the trees formed a canopy of luminous green leaves rustling high above them.

"Is that what it is, Julio? Am I to shatter like eggshells within your fist so that I can finally embrace my true nature?"

Julio motioned for them to sit by the water on a large outcropping of rocks. He put his arms around her and held her close.

"Many times in my life I have lived for the sounds of this water and for the light reflected on its surface. It's so simple to me to be alone. I listen for the high wind in the pines and my heart fills with love and I am truly complete."

"Are you saying that you need no one, not even me?"

"It's not a matter of need. It's all a matter of my relationship with the Great Spirit . . . or what I call power, or what some would call God."

Sin Corazón sat, staring at the water for a long time, feeling their fate already heading downstream with the steady flow of energy.

"What about what you have come here to learn?" she finally asked.

"I don't know that we come here to learn anything," Julio stated matter-of-factly.

"What?" Sin Corazón was stunned by his statement. "How can you say that after all you've learned with your nagual man way?"

"Opening to power and allowing love to become what I am

made of gives me my abilities to make wonderful movements in the world, and that's all. That's not learning to me."

"Aren't we just talking about semantics here, or the softer meanings of words?"

"No. I have never forgotten who I am, and neither have you. You have always been, and always will be, a part of the Great Spirit. You experience that love for the Great Spirit through action. Look at the light gleaming off the water. In that radiance is everything you are looking for."

"For all its beauty, I can't hold and caress it. It's not you, even if it may be the essence of you," Sin Corazón said, emotion welling up inside her. "Can't we walk the path of power together?"

"We can, but not in the way that you think."

"What do you mean?"

"For me to dream and to work I need mostly to be alone. That's the way it has always been. Perhaps that will change, however. I never ask—I just do, and I just am. I don't know any other way."

"You could learn another way." Sin Corazón poked his side, and they both laughed.

As they sat silently together, Sin Corazón wondered at the depth of love and emotion that she felt for Julio. But for all the almost twinlike qualities that they possessed, the basic way Sin Corazón perceived learning and teaching made her see that her form of action was quite different from his. She felt that her path from now on was to help make available to more people this extraordinary world of magic and power. In actuality, this was the first time that this idea had truly occurred to her. She could almost hear Jaguar Woman's voice on the gentle wind, urging her thoughts toward this idea. "Out of loss is created great mysteries of beauty and ability," came a voice from deep inside her. "When our people lost everything, we created another world to go to, and we experience the nagual worlds of beauty and dreaming. We are never born and we never die, and for the spirit there is great comfort in this knowledge.

Share it with those who want to know. This is your new life. You have walked all the trails. Now, help those who begin and who balance precariously on the canyon's edge. You understand how great their fall can be."

The voice was gone, and Sin Corazón looked into Julio's eyes, which were full of the tears of knowing.

XV

Sin Corazón had been walking through the deep forest east
of Tikal, in Petén in Guatemala, toward the border with Belize.
Tikal was an ancestral location for her. Even though most of
the remains were no longer there, she knew the burial grounds
of her ancestors. She could feel the energy there, and at one
time in her life, she had traversed those burial grounds as a
place of power, a place where she could move through the
gateways into the darkness. Now she moved through that area
with love in her heart, even though her heart was breaking,
even though she was beginning to feel that Julio was lost to her,
that there was no hope. There was too much time separating
them, even though she knew that time really did not exist. She
always tested her teachers and their words. She knew she had
to pay her karmic debt. But couldn't there be another way? In
the world of flesh, her heart was breaking because Julio seemed
no longer to be there. But somehow in the alchemy of their love
together, Julio had had the ability to absorb the darkness of her
reflection.

Now as she visited the pyramidal graves of her ancestors,
she healed the self that she had been when she was here before
and she did ceremony, dancing on the graves, dancing on the
energy that had once seduced her. She returned that energy to
its rightful source. She knew that in the grander scheme of
things she had chosen an arduous path toward enlightenment,
but she also realized that her spirit shield must have needed
extraordinary strengthening for her to have asked for this kind
of pain. She knew that she was in danger of losing touch with
her own power. She was in danger of being invaded and being

incorporated into some plan that was not her own.

She remembered Jaguar Woman in the Yucatán years ago when they had been working on shields for the Sisterhood. Jaguar Woman had asked her to make a beautiful shield that represented who she was and her beauty and her power. Sin Corazón had done that well. She had placed it on the ground for Jaguar Woman to see, and one evening Jaguar Woman had come in, carrying her own shield, her face radiant with power. She came over to where Sin Corazón was sitting, proud of her beautiful shield and what it represented; obviously, it was a celebration of who she was. She remembered how Jaguar Woman had taken her shield, had nudged Sin Corazón's shield with a toe, and had placed her shield on top of Sin Corazón's.

"There. What does that remind you of?" Jaguar Woman asked her.

"I don't understand," she said.

Not only had Jaguar Woman placed her shield on top of Sin Corazón's, but she also had ground it down into Sin Corazón's shield with no respect for what Sin Corazón's shield was, the beauty of it, the fragility of it, the perfection of it. She saw Jaguar Woman destroying the perfection of it with her own shield. Then Jaguar Woman stepped onto the shields, grinding them even farther into the dirt, and she said, "Never forget. This is what most people do to each other. They place their shields on top of your own and say that they are theirs. They destroy your vision and ask you to live their own. This is the way of most marriages, of most relationships. Be careful in your life and never give away the power of your shield to someone else."

Then she had gone over and taken her shield off Sin Corazón's and placed it next to Sin Corazón's.

"This is as it should be. Two shields flying through the universe together in perfect harmony and perfect balance."

After a four-day journey, Sin Corazón returned to her small home and spent some time preparing herbs she had gathered

on the way. She spent hours doing ceremony to end her con-
nection to the old sorcerer and thought of Julio and Jaguar
Woman.

A knock at the door separated Sin Corazón from her reverie.
She opened the door to see a small boy with a large envelope
in his hands. He handed it to her and quickly ran away into
the shadows. She took the note and knew instinctively that it
was from Julio. She looked at it, touched it, laid it down on her
table, and sat in front of it for a long time, her eyes closed,
afraid to read the contents. Then as her room became cloaked
in darkness, the sun completely gone from the horizon, her
candle flickering and going out from an overabundance of
wax, she reached out and opened the letter. It had been carefully folded with great attention. She could sense that. She
opened it and took it over to the window so that the last vestiges of waning light could illuminate the page. It was indeed
a note from Julio. She could sense that the note had been written and rewritten many times. As she read his words, she felt a
sinking in her belly. It was not a letter of rejection or farewell,
but it was a letter of engagement. It spoke of a long engagement with loneliness. It was about space and freedom and ultimately, a time of separation. He was saying that he needed
time, that he needed to end certain commitments in his life to
power, that he had never imagined being a householder in this
lifetime and that the mountain within him had told him many
things about the beauty of their love and the strength of their
work together. He felt unequal, he said. He felt that he was losing himself to the sacred dream that they had created between
them, and he had to get stronger. He had to find his way back
to her, he said. For this time, I am in the mountains, he said,
and I am moving from peak to valley in my own soul. I am
searching for an identity that has no name, an identity that
seems to be shimmering just out of reach, an identity that has
always been there but I have denied.

Julio was running, she knew. Could she believe him that he
was running to himself? He was not reinventing himself; he

was reuniting with the truth that represents his spirit in all dimensions of reality. He had separated from that reality long ago, unknowingly, and it wasn't until Sin Corazón had come into his life that he realized that he was a pretender in the world of sorcery, a pretender that had fooled even himself. But he had not fooled Sin Corazón.

Sin Corazón set the letter down, lit a candle, and walked around her adobe hut, beautiful with *nichos* filled with icons, *nichos* newly filled with love, with caring. She cried for a long time. She cried out of her loneliness, out of the separation, out of the vacuum that had been created by his absence, but she also knew that this was not over yet. She knew that she was real, and in the letter that she wrote back to him, she said so, and she said that when he became real, to call for her.

"And what do I do now?" Sin Corazón considered.

She went outside and looked at the towering trees above her, the rubber trees, their broad leaves glistening in the moonlight. Vines flowered on the branches, purple orchids against the darkness, each blossom catching a glint of light from the hovering moon in the cloud-filled sky. She became like the trees for a time. She wandered through the tree branches in her mind, and then standing at the edge of a clearing, a drop of land before her, she focused her intent down around her navel and just below. She spent some time gathering her power and her energy as she had always done, and then slowly she developed a line of energy. Through her intent, her focus, and her power, she sent out a tubelike illumination, a luminous tube that stretched out and down into the deep canyon before her. Then she stretched that tube of energy out across the outcropping of rocks and the low hanging bushes in the moonlight and secured her intent to a giant ceiba tree on the other side of the canyon. Then without any way of explaining what she was doing, she simply began to fly, but in a conscious way, not in a process of dreaming. In her physical body she moved, somehow, into the world of power, through that gateway into the special world where guardians of that domain teach and hover in shimmering light. With her intent and a surge of energy, she moved across the canyon through this tube of luminous fiber that extended from her belly, and she enveloped herself into herself and came out on the other side high in the ceiba tree, looking down at the world before her.

If someone had been in that clearing that night, they would have seen a young jaguar perched in the branches lying there, licking her paws, enjoying the power of her countenance and her ability to reign over the forest. It was the first time that Sin Corazón had used her powers in a long time. Her involvement with Julio had taken her outside of her own world of expertise, and now she felt it time to go back into what she knew, not from a place of darkness, but from a place of enjoyment.

As her power animal, she luxuriated in her process of creation. She leapt down from the branches onto the ground. Was she a woman, was she a cat, was she a medicine cat? Who was she? Who needed to define her identity? Who needed to know of her essence? She had thought to share that essence, that brilliance. Perhaps that had not been such a good idea. Perhaps their chance was over. Perhaps this was all they would ever have. At the thought of that she bounded along a deer trail in the forest, rubbing her back against the low-flung branches, the dampness of the evening drenching her feline fur with dew. She loved her power. She loved her wildness, and she would never be separated from it, not for Julio, not for any man. It was the first time that Sin Corazón really understood that she need not give up her power even though she was giving up the dark side. She was hurting no one as she padded down through this forest path. She was not harming, she was enjoying the science that she had learned, that had been her life. Sin Corazón had realized herself within the matrix and the fibers of love. She realized now that it was time to return to her sisters, to the Sisterhood of the Shields and to her benefactor, Jaguar Woman. It was time to reclaim her position within the world circle of power and creativity.

*   *   *

This time Sin Corazón returned to the Jaguar Temple of the Sun as a woman and not in her dreambody. This time she came with a basket laden with fruit, a huipele, and bread. She brought some liquor and water, sugar and copal, and certain things that were sacred to her teacher. It had been a long journey to arrive at this hidden temple, and for a short time she had had difficulty in finding it because the jungle had overgrown it and it had changed, but soon the energy field attracted her.

It had been days now since she had left Tikal. The sun was warm on her back. There was a dampness in the air, and the ground felt damp and hard beneath her feet. It smelled pungent from the earth. The grasses of the jungle forest were a welcome perfume. Her nostrils filled with it, and it made her heady. She circled the temple, which took some doing through the undergrowth. She began to sing her power song, calling her teacher, calling her. There was a plaintive note to her cadence. Within her melody was a tragic quality that betrayed her pain because there were moments when she missed Julio almost more than she could bear. She had never known a depth of feeling like this. She tried to move her attention away from such feelings, wondering what the fates had in store for her, daring really not to think about it for very long.

She sat in front of where she knew the temple door was, a position in the hill of vines and rubber leaves and molding vegetation. It looked like nothing other than a hill of jungle, giant trees in a canopy overhead, all manner of birds and jungle creatures calling to one another, chirping, laughing, going about their business. She sat in the shade of a rubber tree and waited, moving deep into the center of her consciousness. The day progressed, and she knew that when the moon was at its zenith, Jaguar Woman would come or she would not. As the moon moved to its height in the sky, Sin Corazón became filled with a new energy. Her muscles became taut and ready. She felt the presence of power stalking her. She was not sure of the energy. She was not sure. It has been a long time. She sat back underneath the leaves, watching, ready, ready for anything. Then to her dismay, the foliage around her began to move ever so gently, like a slow earthquake, and to her amazement the roots and the tangled vegetation began to part from the inside, and the ancient temple door, the stones, began to roll aside. Jaguar Woman had been within the temple all this time. Perhaps she has scrutinized the energy fields of her apprentice. Perhaps she has wanted to make Sin Corazón wait and become more ready for this meeting.

Sin Corazón stood up in the moonlight and waited. Candlelight began to flicker in the darkness, and Jaguar Woman stood in the opening, wearing her jaguar mask. Magnificently carved and painted, it was the pure face of power, the most beautiful ceremonial object Sin Corazón had ever seen. It had been within the Sisterhood forever and had been the object of much agitation. The adversaries of the Sisterhood always had wanted to steal it. Red Dog had tried to steal it. It was the pure face of power.

Jaguar Woman played with the energy carefully. She moved her intent and her arms in a certain way, creating a vortex of force with her fingers and hands. She smudged her apprentice with copal. She was dressed in plumes of smoke from the bottoms of her feet to the top of her head. Sin Corazón was crying now. She had not known whether Jaguar Woman would present herself or not. Now she knew that the dream truly had been validated. The words that she had spoken in the dream, she reiterated to Jaguar Woman. She knew that she had been an errant demon, and she couldn't imagine what Jaguar Woman was going to do. Jaguar Woman was not a friendly old grandmother, hapy to see a long-distant child. There was a fierceness in her positioning with Sin Corazón. She knew that she was embarking on a journey that she might not survive.

As they moved into the temple, Sin Corazón felt a kind of fear, and yet she was so resigned to what she had seen within her process of redesigning herself that it seemed as if she had given over to Jaguar Woman as one gives over to her god, and she placed herself into the hands of her teacher.

"I give you this basket, humbly, from my heart with respect, with love, with the grace of transition. I am within your domain. As I said to you before, do with me as you will, for if I come from a place of lack, if I have lost my integrity and my sense of goodness and what is real, then I no longer need to live. I know that you will transform me in whatever way you see fit."

She sat in front of her teacher, her heart completely open, completely vulnerable, in a place of ultimate trust and faith. The guidance of her teacher was of ultimate importance to her, and she knew that Jaguar Woman would do what was correct and appropriate for her evolvement. There was a moment when Jaguar Woman approached Sin Corazón, when Sin Corazón could see that for one predatory moment, her life may have been in danger, as if with one swipe from a giant jaguar paw her identity could have been erased from the face of the earth. But that moment passed, and only love came toward her and enveloped her, as the plumes of smoking copal had enveloped her.

Jaguar Woman removed her mask and placed it on an altar step to her right and lit a candle. Sin Corazón observed her face. There was more than some fear in her heart for this woman. She knew that she had incurred not only her compassion but also her wrath. Jaguar Woman, her ancient face seeming to smooth beneath the light streaming in from a circular indentation in the ceiling of the cavern, did not look at her apprentice but closed her eyes to move into the extraordinary universe within her own soul. Her hair, snow white, was pulled back in a knot at the nape of her neck. Her bronzed skin seemed luminescent and alive with sparkling energy.

As Jaguar Woman began to speak her whole body seemed to shimmer and become translucent. For a moment Sin Corazón thought that she might become transparent before her eyes, that somehow she was moving into other worlds and had chosen, perhaps, to end this relationship with her, but as

Jaguar Woman spoke, Sin Corazón became more assured that her teacher was still here for her.

"For all that you have done in this world," Jaguar Woman said slowly in a deep voice unlike any other Sin Corazón had heard, as if it came from lifetimes away from this moment, "the path that you chose, my daughter"—the use of that term brought tears to Sin Corazón's eyes; she had not heard it in this way for so very many years—"your path of darkness took you into the roots of the jungle of mystery, took you deep into the underworld. Did you meet the beings of the underworld that you wished to meet?" Now she opened her eyes and looked at Sin Corazón.

Sin Corazón thought for some time about her question. "Yes," she finally said. "I met many mysterious allies in that world. I met them and I danced with them, and I have left them. I have no ties there any longer. I have no agreements in the world of darkness that cannot be met or that I need to perform."

Jaguar Woman knew of what she spoke. She knew of the agreements that are made between energy forms, not only within this lifetime but also in the nagual worlds of power. She breathed deeply with this knowledge. She got up from her seat of forgetting and remembering. She wandered, seemingly aimlessly, around the cavern for many minutes, and then she turned and with extraordinary intensity looked at Sin Corazón, who jumped back physically from the strength of her gaze.

"But you do have one agreement left," Jaguar Woman said.

Sin Corazón was afraid to ask what that might be, and for a moment she felt so extraordinarily ignorant that she became confused.

"Ah," Jaguar Woman said. "I can see your confusion. Remember, my daughter, that whatever path you tread, perhaps the only evil in this life is confusion. If you are in a war with another being and you fight with the knives of light and darkness, if you pause for one moment in that state of confu-

sion, it may be your last moment because that is the kind of
vulnerability that you cannot afford. It is not a good shield like
the shield that is created through innocence. You have one
agreement left. By the very fact that you chose the dark road of
sorcery, you must remember that you never take or create anything in this world that you do not have to pay for. And now
you have to pay for your choice at that crossroads so long ago.
That choice came from your own indulgence. Your indulgence
was your pain. Your indulgence was your grief. There is no
grief that could ever warrant what you did, my daughter. Not
that I do not understand. Not that I do not have compassion
for your experiences. But this is truth, and it is law. For all that
you have done, you have lived through the karma of that
doing. But your choice has not yet been paid for."

Sin Corazón was crying now. She felt the deep pain and
weight of her teacher's words. Jaguar Woman sat now again,
her head held high in a position of authority, the painful goddess when she knows that retribution must be served. She sat
in the circle of eternal law. She sat in the position of the sacred
zero, and she knew that all things are added up and collected
through time and through history, that all things have a sum.

Sin Corazón stopped crying. She collected herself and sat
before her teacher, thinking that perhaps the retribution was
certain death. But as the silence continued, she realized that
she needed to find the answer somewhere within herself. She
moved past her terror. She moved around the wild thoughts
of lifelong agonies that could be done to her, such as even her
teacher leaving her to her own demise, which certainly would
be the worst thing that she could think of. And then with a
gasp, she realized what it was. She faced her teacher in such
pain that she did not know if she could survive, or if she
would want to.

Reading her thoughts, Jaguar Woman said very quietly,
"You must live, you will live, and you will learn to love
another day." For it was Julio who could not be in her life as
she had dreamed. Jaguar Woman wanted her to deepen with

her grief so that perhaps finally she could allow true love with Julio actually to occur. Otherwise, they would be lost to each other forever.

Sin Corazón could not believe for a moment how this had come around full circle. "But Jaguar Woman, this is where I lost my way so long ago. It was through my grief over my husband. How can it be that this is to happen again?"

"Because you did not learn your lesson the first time," the old woman said. "And this whole life is lessons until we are sick of them, until we no longer want to learn those lessons, until we want to run screaming into the night, but learn these lessons we must. There is no other way. This is what we have chosen on this physical plane. We do not come here, my daughter, to be happy, to be peaceful, to be simply wondrous beings of light. We become those wondrous beings of radiance when we have grown and learned the lessons we came here to learn. You think that I have not suffered? You think that I have become this woman of wisdom without many forked trails?"

Sin Corazón looked at her and nodded, her stomach feeling as if a mule had kicked her.

"I understand, my teacher."

She sat up straight, tears washing her cheeks, and leaned forward, as if she were placing her head on the stone bench of Chacmul, in preparation for the ancient Mayan blood sacrifice. She felt that if her head were removed, if her heart were taken from her breast, that it would have hurt the same, but then it would have been over. But this would never be over, and she knew it. She also knew that she must take this journey like a warrioress—strong, powerful, and proud—that she had been given, in fact, another chance.

"I must know one thing. Is it possible that all of this was designed by the Sisterhood? Is it possible that not only my husband but also Julio were placed in my life to test me in some way?" The horror of this thought was more than Sin Corazón wished to think of for long.

Jaguar Woman laughed out loud. She laughed deeply and

then very seriously began to address her apprentice. "There is nothing in this life that is not by some grand design. There is always a bigger picture to everything that happens to us, but to think that you or anyone is so important that others' lives would be completely altered for great, long periods of time simply for your instruction is, of course, unthinkable. But it is also true that there is an agreement on other levels of reality made among all the people whom you have ever known throughout your history as a being.

"As your spirit shield flies through the universe, collecting the dusts of creation and experience, there is always an agreement. There is always something to be learned so that the spirit shield can be imprinted with even more power and evolvement. So to think that your spirit shield is spinning away into the worlds of light and darkness without thought, without direction, without there being the powers of the gods and the goddesses surrounding you, is folly as well.

"It is unthinkable to imagine that the Sisterhood of the Shields or any other gathering of people of wisdom would ensnare you in such a diabolical fashion as you have been snared with the old sorcerer. There has been a net of fibers around you that have encased your experience, but that fabric was of your own weaving and design. None other but you is responsible for the challenges that you have created. You have created them and there have been agreements, but these all energetically and within the physical world have been your choice. It was appropriate for me to see Julio and to provide you the opportunity to meet with him as you did. From then on it was your decision. I see his energy lines and I see yours. I am a counter of time throughout history. I count your time, your incarnations, abilities, and I help you to realize that which you cannot see but desire—not wanting in physical, worldly riches, but in the wanting of the spirit.

"I am Jaguar Woman because a long time ago, when our people were destroyed, the spirit lived on in the jaguar, it is told. I live on as the spirit of my people. I am Jaguar Woman.

You, my daughter, carry that spirit as your ally. You toy with the physical, but in spirit this journey is very serious, and ultimately, deep with humor."

Jaguar Woman reached out her hands to Sin Corazón, took them, and brought her close to her and held her in a short embrace. Darkness had enshrouded the temple in shadows. But shafts of first morning light now replaced the moonshine that seemingly only minutes before had been reflecting off Jaguar Woman's forehead. Her aquiline nose now reflected the fading stars. Her skin, dark from the sun, seemed dark blue, like the stars that she knew so well, their light permeating her shields of spirit, her skin, their knowledge being her knowledge, the ancient history of her people written across the lines in her face and her hands. She had given her words to her apprentice, but she had given no instruction.

"It is not time," she said simply. "It is not time for you to do other than sit in the center of your own circle of power and explore the directions of your life, explore your shields, explore the crossroads that you sit at in this moment in time. You have many decisions to make, and they must come from the deepest integrity that you know. So return to your village. Return to your dreaming. Strengthen your dreambody, my daughter, for you will need it in the days to come. I will visit you. You do not need to seek me out again. I will visit you in your dreaming, and I will come to you in many ways in the days of this moon. You will see me and we will work together. We will retrieve the pieces of your spirit that are flying around aimlessly in the universe, looking for their home. I am full with my love for you."

She put her hand into a fist, and she touched her heart. Sin Corazón closed her eyes and bowed her head in ultimate respect for her teacher. She knew that she would see Jaguar Woman soon, and she had much work she needed to do quietly and within the silence of her own being.

XVI

Sin Corazón sat within herself, waiting, and she began to grow
cool. In her coolness the reality of her relationship with Julio,
her life as it had been, became even more clear, like stars in a
melancholy sky—clear, sparkling, impenetrable, and untouch-
able. What she wanted of life seemed out of reach, like those
stars in the distance, and yet their brightness was so clear, it
was as if they were a part of her. At moments, her thoughts
would race through her mind, and she would think of what
could be her life now with her love for Julio. But then why did
he not come to her?

Why was there this distance? Was she to learn something
she wasn't seeing? Or was Jaguar Woman saying she would
never see Julio again? It was not as if Julio's energy had been
pulled away, but rather as if the energy was becoming stagnant, settling in, not moving one way or another. As a sorceress, she knew that once the energy is stagnant, it begins to
lose its power and its thrust, and life begins to leave you. She
wondered if the old sorcerer had gotten to him. She knew that
her instinct was to run, to become angry, to lash out, to hurt
Julio; or her other alternative, perhaps, was just simply to
leave him forever without saying good-bye. But with that
thought it seemed as if darkness was again infringing on her
being. Leaving without closing the circle would be to lose
what she had learned and worked so hard to gain. People
think that they can control one another, but in actuality in the
depths of things, no one can control anyone other than herself. In controlling another person, you lose the very thing
that you desired because in controlling people you are never

really sure if they would be there on their own.

Sin Corazón was giving Julio enough rope to hang himself. She was giving him the space to fill or leave empty. Julio, on the other hand, she thought, may be doing the same thing— waiting for her in some way. But she felt that Julio must make the next move, forgetting the plays of power and energy. It was essential for her to respect him as a man, and to love him. Yet somewhere deep in her heart she was losing respect for Julio. Somehow she felt that she had found his weakness, and instead of acting as a sorceress and moving into that weakness to see what she could find, she stayed away. Instead of wanting harm or control or revenge, she sat within her love, watching the turmoil and the chaos and the procession of nature as it develops, ebbs and flows, dies, and is reborn. She felt the birth of the universe within her heart. She felt the stars and the sun and the moon in their transit. She felt the beginning of life and vegetation, the love and the instinct of animals, the selfishness, the greed, the joy of humanness, and all within her own soul. She felt as if she had lain down on the floor with her feet against a wall. She felt that she had cast her legs in such a way that she could no longer get up.

In another self that stood proud and strong and unafraid, she simply waited, not as a target waits for the arrow to strike, but for this teaching to become clear.

After all these years, she was beginning to trust again, after all these years, in the goodness of her spirit, in the power of the Great Spirit and the Goddess Mother and all of the things that Jaguar Woman had taught her. She began to relax as the images of her love for Jaguar Woman and her love for other people in her life long ago came to her. She began to realize that in a sense there is nothing any of us can do to make things happen, to make things quit. We can move away from abuse, from harm, from impending danger, but in affairs of the heart, when love is within you and shared, then you wait in many ways.

XVII

Jaguar Woman sat under an enormous stand of jungle trees and looked at Sin Corazón with her piercing eyes, the way she did when she wanted to make a point. "To make a choice is to divide your power. In a sense, there is no choice ever; there is only a oneness of love in the universe." She stood up, and taking a branch from a tree, she separated it from the trunk with a loud crack.

"Now," she said, "is the tree stronger?"

"In some cases, yes," Sin Corazón had said. "And in some cases, no."

"Correct," Jaguar Woman said, "but even if you separate the branch from the tree, you have still not separated the oneness of all life from itself. When you make a choice between one man or another, you are not making a choice against the oneness of life. You are making a choice that has to do with your integrity and who you are in the world. You do not make a choice depending on what they feel. You make a choice depending upon who you feel that you are in this world."

Sin Corazón was experiencing the feeling of yielding, simply yielding to the forces within the universe, the forces that animate our life, called destiny, called the Great Spirit. She was allowing that force to wander through her as a stranger in an unknown house, and yet this force was no stranger to her. But her attitude about it was different and unknown to her until this moment. Her point of view had changed, and she realized that one of the most important things that she had ever experienced was the power of a point of view. It sounded so simple, she laughed to herself. In changing a point of view, life changes from darkness to magic, from weakness and pain to power and tranquility. Instead of yearning for Julio and the agony of missing him and his touch, she moved into caressing her own wounded spirit, nourishing herself, loving herself beyond all boundaries. Then suddenly there was no harm. There was no yearning. There was only space and waiting. If that space were never filled again, there was only the blissfulness of her experience of the Great Spirit within herself. And Julio had been a true reflection of that majesty and the depth of what true love and spirit can be.

All of her began to relax. Sin Corazón relaxed into a sense of knowingness—not that knowingness was defined into words or sentences or any kind of structure. It was a wisdom of formlessness that came upon her like a cloud moving off the horizon. She lay back with a sense that the arms of the Great Mother were holding her, protecting her, not only from Julio but also from herself and a point of view that had been dangerous and incorrect and painful. She knew at last that the goodness within her own soul could manifest into the world. She could make the world whatever she wanted it to be, depending on how she saw the reality happening all around her. She could see the light or she could live in the dark—the darkness formed by her attitudes about life and how she perceived the actions of the one she loved.

XVIII

The mountain stood majestic, silhouetted in black and purple and gold in the evening sky. Trees moved gently in the evening breeze. Everything was the same. The trees were singing. The birds were singing. The earth was damp and warm. The air that she breathed was the same as it had been yesterday and as it would be tomorrow. But time stood still for her now as she sat in front of Julio, who had arrived unannounced and unexpected. She had dreamed that she would not see him again for a long time. Inside her body her energy was quaking like a giant eucalyptus in a strong wind, but on the outside she was serene and collected and listening. Julio, on the other hand, seemed disheveled and strange. His hair seemed unkept. His skin was clean and yet seemed not altogether healthy. His clothes were washed but wrinkled, and he looked as if he had been traversing his interior world with difficulty. She wanted to reach out to him, to hold him, to make him feel more comfortable, and yet something held her back. In a sense there was a deep anger at the pain that she was feeling, an anger at the source of her being. But she said nothing and waited for his words, which seemed difficult in coming. Julio looked away at the dark horizon of clouds and certain thunderstorm nearing San Cristóbal. A strong beam of light emanated from the clouds and illuminated a peak in the mountains, shining emerald green and yellow and orange. He looked toward that peak and he wished that he were on it, soaking up the last vestiges of sun, deep within meditation and power. Then he whirled around to look at Sin Corazón with such love in his eyes that it brought tears to her own.

"I am caught in a dilemma," he finally said.

Sin Corazón nodded. "And I share that dilemma," she said simply.

"I have been lost in a doorway, a wrinly in time," he said. "I have dreamt that forever I could walk the hallways, the pathways of dreaming, keep my physical body and live in my spiritual body. But you have changed me. When I absorbed your reflection in the pond that night, when the magic of the gods surrounded us and touched us, you were not the only one who was absorbed. I, too, seem to have made some agreement that I do not understand."

"There are ancient gods of blood sacrifice," Sin Corazón said. "I have been laid many times onto the altars of that sacrifice. I have been the one who wielded the blade, and I have been the victim, but never," she said, "have I experienced the anguish I feel at this time. And I, too, do not understand why love should create such pain."

Julio breathed deeply and reached a hand out to Sin Corazón and touched her fingers and stroked them gently and held them first to his forehead and then to his heart.

"There are things I must tell you," he said. "It is not often in many lifetimes that you meet someone who is ready."

Sin Corazón raised her eyebrows, as if in question. Julio's face was beginning to brighten, and his skin was beginning to smooth before her eyes. "It is not often that someone is ready · to be touched, and I am touching you."

"What do you mean?" Sin Corazón said.

"I am changing you."

For a long time their eyes met. Sin Corazón searched with her true ability to see. She was looking for a hint of darkness, of manipulation. She was not altogether sure that she did not see that shadow somewhere on the periphery of her vision.

Finally Julio siad, "You are being challenged."

Then Sin Corazón sat back, as if pushed.

"What are you doing to me?" she asked, surprised by his use of words. She was very unaccustomed to feeling as if anybody ever was doing anything to her. She watched the play of light across his face, emblazoned now with a very seductive smile. She wondered at that kind of attention being used toward her. She was unaccustomed to that expression on his face. It was not a pure expression, and she was tantalized by that and set back by that at the same time.

"Your spine is like a ladder of light," he said, "and within your spine there are keys and wheels, and sometimes when you are accompanied by great love, you can turn those keys and a door is opened and a process is begun. Once it has begun, there is no stopping it."

Instead of being warmed by his words, Sin Corazón was concerned.

"Julio, are you trying to indoctrinate me in some way?" She was on the edge of real anger.

"There is no indoctrination when you are talking about the Great Spirit," he said gently. The look of intrigue had passed from his face. His gaze was perfectly clear.

"Then what," she demanded, "are you saying?"

"I have never put this into words," Julio said. "I am doing it badly, but I want you to understand perfectly what is happening here. You know that I am talking about something very special—the nagual, which is so beyond the physical world, beyond our physical understanding."

"Yes," Sin Corazón said, calming herself. This man whom she loved so much was traversing a terrain unfamiliar even to him.

Obviously in deep thought, Julio traced circles in the dirt with a stick, over and over, finally taking the stick and stabbing it into the center of the circle. He looked at her and very simply said, "I am illuminating you."

Sin Corazón was stunned with the presumptuousness of his statement.

"But what does this all have to do with us walking down the path together? What does this have to do with our love?"

Julio stared at her for a long time. There was silence

between them as the sun slid from the horizon and the shadows grew long and melted into one another, into a curtain of darkness that surrounded them like a cocoon, soft, perfumed, and delicate. "I have never been out of control in my life, " he said, "whether that is good, or whether it is bad. And now I feel out of control. That is my demon. That is what faces me because I cannot control the wildness of your soul."

"And I cannot control yours," Sin Corazón said, "nor do I wish to."

"Ah!" Julio exclaimed. "But we are made of power, you and I. So how can this not be a game of power?"

"But if this is a game, Julio, then we both lose. If you crush me, you, as a healer, will be crushed with the memory of me. And if you are crushed, then I, too, could not go on, and we would lose each other, one way or another. Whether you win or you lose, we both lose in a game of power."

"But that is the dilemma that faces us. There are more powers here than just you and me."

For a moment Sin Corazón had a vision of a temple of priestesses and Mayan robes, feathers, sacrificial bowls of blood. She felt a stabbing pain in her gut when she thought of the wars that the Sisterhood of the Shields and so many brotherhoods and sisterhoods around the earth are fighting against ignorance and pain, darkness and stupidity. She thought how blood sacrifice had continued long past the Mayan and Aztec days into wars and bloodlettings of every imaginable kind. She ached for those who, somehow, had missed their opportunities to emerge into the light.

Then she looked at this man she loved. Holding his face in her hands, she said simply, "We are only transformed by the process of love. It's all we have, and it's all that we are. Without that, we have nothing and we are nothing."

XIX

Julio had been climbing the red sandstone mesa for an hour.
Every step had been precarious and slippery, as tiny pebbles
would roll away from beneath his boots. When he reached the
summit he was surprised to see that the plateau of the mesa
was long, perfectly flat, windblown, and only about four feet
wide. He sat down and faced the western gateway as the
orange, fiery hot sun hung low in the sky.

Julio felt a longing inside. He was unaccustomed to intense
feelings of this kind. He ached to regain his center. The wind
picked up from the south. A small dust devil funneled several
tumbleweeds hundreds of feet into the afternoon sky. Julio
sighed, trying to release the emotional pain in his gut. He
smiled to himself. He realized once again that no matter how
deeply he loved, maybe nothing, even this, would touch the
brittle edges of his heart. For so long he had shielded himself
from vulnerability. Then, throwing his head back, he laughed
out loud, sharing the song of two ravens flying high in the air
drafts above him. Of course, why hadn't he seen it before. José,
his teacher, had often mentioned this to him. Your best defense
is your own vulnerability. He hadn't been vulnerable. Perhaps
he never could be. Great Spirit preserve my sanity, he prayed.
He felt tormented, and yet he was not touched in the deepest
places within his being. He was not touched by her, then why
or how could he be so in love? He bent double, his forehead
touching his knees. When he saw the beautiful face of Sin
Corazón in his mind, it was as if a hook were being pulled
through his body. Like a fish being caught, he wriggled his
consciousness away from her. He would not lose himself to

her. He would not lose his way of life. It was not that he was frightened, he was not to be controlled. With that thought, he stood up in the hot wind. His eyes had turned bright red with the reflection of the setting sun. With a smile coming from some inner place of joy, Julio leapt off the mesa and into the air, half-running, half-tumbling into the squatting, skiing position he knew so well. Landing on his left foot, he held his right leg in front of him as a rudder as he skied down the slippery sandstone at almost the speed of free fall. He was skiing on his feet with perfect balance. At this very moment he felt completely alive. There was nothing else in existence but him and his god. Nothing could touch him now as he sped down the giant mesa in the lingering red light of sunset. Julio was an edge man, a man who pushed the limits of his physical endurance and the boundaries of his reality every chance he got. It was at those special moments that the orgasm of creativity and life force became one within him, and at last he felt touched by the invisible fingers of the great mystery that surrounded him. Julio felt free, Julio felt alive, Julio was close to death.

XX

Julio had left for Veracruz, and Sin Corazón had been traveling to her various places of power. She used his name like a mantra, repeating it over and over to lead her into the state of dreaming that was so familiar to her. She used his name and she used other names of power that took her into the sacred valley of her spirit.

She also journeyed into a very special power place called Gaianos. This valley is so female, so feminine in its power. She walked through a lush clearing with ceiba trees and damp, dark earth beneath her feet. She heard the sound of the creek rushing by. There had been plenty of rain that winter, and she knew that there was plenty of water for the fish and the wildlife that lived nearby. She walked through the clearing, and she knew that there was something there for her. There is a teaching, an understanding, a wisdom, a message some-where high in the branches of the trees or in the stones or in the breath of air that moves the leaves and the tree branches swinging like the long hair on Julio's head.

Then she looked up to the far north of the valley. She saw a giant mountain lifting up, a mesa covered with piñon, scrub pine, and rock granite at the summit. She realized that this val-ley, so feminine in its countenance, had a powerful male pres-ence in this mountain. This is not a grandmother mountain. This is a grandfather, a warrior, a medicine mountain, there to teach her and all people who wish to climb it or sit at its feet and listen. Still, there was something eluding her.

She wandered through the valley, slept there that night, and the next morning she crossed over into the forest, walking up

toward the sleeping mesa towering above her. Whatever the
message she was to find, she had missed the forked trails.
Again she called to her own heart, to her teachers, to her
guardians, to her ancestors and to all those who love her to
help her. Again, she used his name; she liked the sound of it,
like a high wind whistling through the pines. More than her
love for him, the power in his name intrigued her, and she
knew that as much as Julio had been in her life, it was extraordinary love that had led her down such a strange and transfor-
mative path.

There was more to this, but she could not seem to find the
missing piece. As a result she was bouncing off the walls of
energy, walking through the forest, ricocheting off the trees
like a low tone, like the sound of the drum, as the heartbeat of
Mother Earth ricochets off the stars in the universe back to us
with even fuller force, urging us to go on, to search, and eventually to find our purpose.

As the sun began to fade on the horizon, Sin Corazón found
a clearing under some poplar trees. Poplars, she thought. I
must be quite high. No wonder it is so cool. She curled up on a
patch of grass near a warm stone that had been heated by the
sun. She curled up like an animal waiting for her mate and
went into a deep sleep. That night she dreamt of her teacher,
and she asked for a teaching.

She assumed her jaguar spirit body and paced through the
night along the trails of darkness and light illuminated by the
moon. A new ring of power was at hand, she realized, that
meant a new level of wisdom different from anything she had
ever known. It was not a wisdom to be acquired but a wisdom
of letting go, of just waiting in silence and peace. In her dreaming she knew that her teaching ancestors and those incarnate
in this lifetime were around, protecting and testing her; could
she find the missing piece? So many things, so many people,
were approaching her. Jaguar Woman, there was Lynn from
the North, Agnes Whistling Elk, Butterfly Woman in her
dreams—all these beings of the light were now beckoning to

her to change, to grow, to become what she had been intended to be. There was a tug on her solar plexus. She knew that she needed to build a new cord for dreaming, something new had to be instated into her energy field so that more possibilities could occur. She had to move certain aspects of her energy field so that that could happen.

Her heart opened with tremendous love, and she saw Julio standing within. She loved him with everything that she knew, but now it seemed even that was not enough. This was about being changed and growing, yet learning nothing—in fact, learning less. A new voice of power was being heard, but she needed a translator, for she had never heard it before.

Through the night she waited in her dreaming, and she saw in the eyes of her jaguar self something she had not noticed before. It was a certain light because the eyes of her jaguar self had been more opaque, dark pools of strength and predatory power. Now there was a light, a softer glint behind all of that strength, an outward pressure that meant a coolness, a sweetness, and a deep love that did not require, necessarily, an object but simply a state of being that occurs within very special nagual women, beings of power on this earth and in other realities.

As she slept she began to move into the beam of light that emanated from the corners of the jaguar's eyes, and she followed that light as if she were someone walking down a path in a forest. Its source was so bright, golden, and radiant beyond comprehension. Would she be burnt to ashes? But that was all right because out of the ashes comes the phoenix. She knew that somewhere in this light was the answer, finally, the piece of the puzzle that she needed for pure balance. She continued to journey until dawn.

"Yield to love. Love yourself and your sisters in your forgetting and remembering. The spirit of our people lives on with you," whispered the voice of power. But the voice was male, and she knew it well. Sin Corazón woke with terror, opening her eyes to see the old sorcerer standing above her. He was surrounded by a fine mist that was beginning to swirl gently with the warmth of the rising sun. "Those are the words you wanted to hear, weren't they? What made you think you could just vanish from my life? You owe me, and I will tell you how you can settle our accounts together. You want your Julio? Then you must give me something in return!"

12
Luminous Gateway

The setting sun shone through the Chilean mesquite tree, making it appear to be green lace filigree, blowing in the wind. The south wind was luxurious, like fine linen on my skin. As I lay in a hammock at Jaguar Woman's house, I could not get Sin Corazón out of my mind. She seemed so truly sorry for the tremendous confusion she had caused us all, to say nothing of the pain that she felt for her own lost years. How we change! I thought. How we become fascinated by people in worlds unknown to us. My mind would wander off onto city streets I had only glimpses of, mountaintops and mesas where Sin Corazón must have moved in her mysterious journey. I thought of her stalking. I had heard tales about her embodiment of the jaguar as her ally. An aspect of me was awed by this extraordinary woman, but I also felt tremendous gratitude to my own guardians for protecting me from such a decision in my own life.

The next day another note arrived from Sin Corazón, asking me to meet her again at the morning market, this time much earlier in the day. Full of expectation, I had to laugh to myself at how I always seemed to tempt the fates one way or another. The sun, orange and golden, rising over the marketplace, roosters crowing, dogs barking, the business of market, and a Mexican town awakening were beautiful. I bought a cup of coffee—something I rarely drink—and sat down on a ledge to watch the colorful play of people. When Sin Corazón appeared, she seemed even younger than when I had seen her last. "Well," she said, toasting my coffee with her own. She stood in a silhouette to the sun, looking like a slender icon, Madonna-like in her cotton shawl draping down to her waist. With her long hair fringing out around her face, she seemed like a very young girl.

"You are pushing the edges, aren't you, Lynn? You've always done that." She laughed. "How have you managed to keep your innocence and not get caught in a snare?"

For a moment she was terrifying. I gulped my coffee and then had to laugh with her, because it was true.

"I am surprised you met me this morning. I thought surely you would be back halfway to Mérida by now."

I looked into the reflection of the golden clouds in the dark liquid of my cup for several moments.

"I wondered, Sin Corazón, if I could ever possibly forgive you completely. The only way I could ever do that is to see you because I cannot forgive you in my mind. I can only forgive you in my heart. I cannot pretend that I did not miss our friendship dearly. How can I ever be your friend again? I can only love you, but I don't know that I could ever trust you."

"But is it a matter of trust?" Sin Corazón said, not even looking at me. "Perhaps evil is simply a fact, a state of being. Trust is a state of being, too, and I think that you're made of trust," she said simply.

"What is it that you want from me, really? I know there is something you need. I can feel it," I said.

"I thought maybe in seeing you again it would be made clear to me as well. I need balance. I have come from darkness and I need so desperately the light. You are made of light, it seems. And so I need your light to balance my darkness."

I was quite surprised at her openness. "But Sin Corazón, isn't that what sorcery is? It's using friendship for gain, something that perhaps the other person does not know about. In friendship, you give love and understanding and light, but you give it knowingly. I will consider it, and am honored that you would think to ask me, but I don't know what I can give that to you. Perhaps some of the other women would be more skilled. Perhaps only Jaguar Woman can work with you now."

I looked at the windows of the buildings around the plaza.

For how many years—decades—had those windows reflected the blood red and pink light of the sun, just as they were reflecting it now? What dramas of life and death, light and darkness, had walked beneath those windows during these many years? What had brought us here to this present reckoning of spirit, of pain and joy? What was to happen to Sin Corazón, and what was the lesson here for me? She was a sorcerer, all right. Already I wanted to give her what she needed.

"Come. Let's take a walk," Sin Corazón suggested.

We walked a short distance around the south end of the marketplace. Women in beautiful colored cotton skirts and blouses and with sleek black hair pulled back from their tanned faces smiled at us and showed us the grain, corn, or leather goods they had for sale. The brilliant sunlight created sharp, distinct shadows behind the town buildings. Along the left side of the plaza were stone steps that had been partly eaten away by time. I noticed an old man sitting against the wall of a pink building. His head was down as if he were sleeping. He was wearing black trousers and a black shirt, and he seemed very old. I couldn't take my eyes away from him. He looked up as if he sensed my stare, and his eyes startled me. They were not the eyes of an old man; they were yellow and piercing underneath his heavy lids. He stood up with unusual agility and smiled mostly on the left side of his lips and looked at me with startling presence. He turned and went through an ancient weathered doorway I had not noticed before. For a moment I was not sure if the door had actually opened or not, but it was closed now as I faced it. I turned quickly to Sin Corazón and caught her watching with an odd smile on her face.

"What an interesting old man!" she said. "Let's follow him. Perhaps this doorway leads to worlds unknown to you."

A chill went up my spine. "That's a gateway, isn't it?" I asked.

"Why, yes, Little Wolf," she said in a too familiar way. "Surely your teachers have trained you how to move through the gateways."

I wanted to run through the plaza and away from this woman, and yet I was fascinated by this gateway at the south end of the plaza. I remembered Ruby warning that I would be in great danger if Sin Corazón moved into the south. But my thoughts were hazy. Surely this was just coincidence! Ruby's words seemed distant and meaningless. I would risk almost anything to learn something knew, and so I stepped forward with Sin Corazón, making the choice that I could handle myself in any situation. And I wanted to follow that old man. He had enticed me, fascinated me. If he were Sin Corazón's teacher, I understood why she had gone with him. For a moment I imagined flying through the air in my energy body and seeing strange magical visions of life and power different from what I had experienced with the Sisterhood. Just as I reached the doorway, the wood around it now vibrating bluish green in the intense morning light, I stopped short. Sin Corazón, because I knew that it was law, had to send me ahead first. Had she gone through the doorway, the energy would have pulled me through, perhaps, against my will—and that would not have served her. What she needed was for me to make the choice.

I came to the doorway and touched it with my hand. My fingers tingled, as if the doorway were made of pure oscillating energy that caressed my fingers in the gentlest, most sublime way. I jumped back, knocking Sin Corazón to the side. She took my shoulders in both her hands and turned me to look at her.

"Wolf Woman, surely you are not afraid of knowledge? There are many things that your teachers have not told you."

"What do you mean?" I asked.

"The dark side of sorcery is not evil, it is the core of personal power. You have treaded on only the circumference of the sacred circles of wisdom. I am offering you a chance to move beyond your limits, into a world so magnificent that you cannot even imagine it. It is not filled with devils with pitchforks and horns, it is filled with angels—with light like you have never seen. In this sky, there are no clouds. The power is like lightning separating the sky into shards of mystery and magic. Follow me, and you'll have power over all people. You will be able to make them do what you will. Think what that would mean in your world, with your work. We have the ability to give you so much."

Now I recoiled from her! I realized the mistake I had almost made, fascinated as I was by the old man. Of course he was fascinating, and so was Sin Corazón's mesmerizing beauty as she stood silhouetted against the sun, her magnificent eyes glistening with passion and power. But I had to see what darkness looked like as it reflected from her eyes, and I saw it very clearly.

It was pure ugliness. I saw the sadness just below the surface, the pain, and the separation from other forms of life. She existed alone in a bubble irresistible and magnificent in form, but its essence was dangerous and destructive.

Our vibrations did not merge. My shields within me were spinning as I built my defense against her seductive ways. And as I spun to the right, she spun to the left, and we bounced off each other. "My God, the south," I almost whispered aloud.

Then Sin Corazón turned away from me with a bitter smile.

"What a shame," she said, "that you are so weak and unknowing. I thought you were more."

She turned with a swirl of her black skirt, like smoke from a dying fire, and she passed through the gateway. Again I was unsure whether the door had actually opened or not.

I hurried across the plaza, almost running, and sat on a stone rim of a beautiful garden filled with roses and bright yellow daisies. For a long time, I centered myself, trying to make sure that none of her energy field was left in mine. I was sitting in the westerly direction of the plaza, caressing the Rainbow Mother shield within me with every thankful breath.

But still I had a sense of foreboding. This dance was not over yet.

13

A Sorcerer's Love

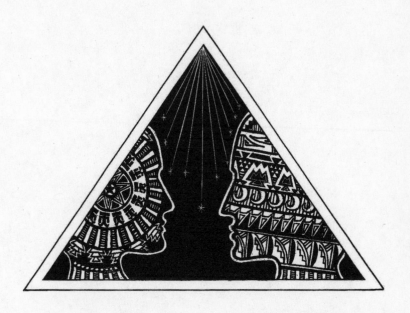

The next day, after we had discussed my meeting with Sin Corazón, we all sat together.

"I think Sin Corazón made one last attempt for her teacher," Jaguar Woman said.

"What do you mean?"

"She wanted to offer you to her teacher in exchange for her own freedom."

That had not occurred to me, but of course she was right.

"That gateway shimmers in the light, doesn't it?" Jaguar Woman asked.

"Yes, and so does the old man," I said.

Jaguar Woman and I stared at each other for a moment. As I realized what I almost had done, perspiration broke out on my forehead. I left the room and sat down on the cool earth outside. After a while, Ruby joined me, sitting next to me.

"It's okay, Lynn. You didn't open that door."

"Ruby, why do I feel as if that was one of the most important moments of my life?"

"Because it was. Now you know who you truly are, not only what you are *not*. Now you have the key."

"What key?"

"Now you can begin to read what is in the clay pots. We needed to hear this from you. You have done well."

"I can? Just like that?"

"Yes, just like that."

I stared at the sky through the trees.

"No matter what you have learned, there is always more," I said.

"Yes. Come." Ruby stood up and reached out a helping hand. We joined the others.

"How does a sorceress fall in love?" I asked Jaguar Woman.

"Well, for one thing," Ruby said, "it is certainly different from the way you or I fall in love—well, different from the way *you* fall in love, maybe." Ruby laughed at the look of surprise on my face.

"What do you mean exactly?" I asked.

"A regular person," Agnes interjected, "who is not involved in the world of power, goes through a courtship. I am talking about the ordinary run-of-the-mill love affair. People meet, they are attracted, they go through a courtship, and they begin to live together, and they get married and make a commitment, usually for life. Although they may not keep that commitment, that is usually the thought at the time."

"But I've seen very few people of power who are householders."

"That's true," Jaguar Woman said. "Zoila and José are both householders, which is a very difficult thing to do because of the nature of their work. They are completely involved in personal power, so anything that keeps them from that personal power is something that ordinarily they would get rid of."

"Do you mean children?"

"Yes, anything. That means, oftentimes, as it has been described, personal history of any kind."

"How I've always understood this, Jaguar Woman, is that if you are a sorcerer or person of power who travels the dimensions of the universe in different ways—through dreaming, through stalking, through healing abilities—then you don't use your energy for other things. It's sort of like being a priest, or a nun who becomes a bride of Christ, for instance. She doesn't bleed off their energy in any other way with relationships in the actual world. Is that what you're saying?"

"This is correct. You become, in a sense, married to power. It is your entire life, and it is a fascinating and mysterious and challenging game."

"A game?" I said.

"Yes, in a sense it's a play of energies and powers and how well you can choreograph those energies. You devote yourself to it completely, and it becomes not unlike a game in the fast lane on Wall Street or in your world of politics. You know other people of power, and if you are a dark sorcerer, you take power from them. You figure out ways to trick them and play games and entice them into boxed canyons. That's what dark sorcery is about, stealing power from someone else. Not a good way to go," she emphasized. "This is the boxed canyon that Sin Corazón found herself in."

"Now," Agnes interrupted, "Sin Corazón and Julio fell in love, truly in love. You must understand that when we sent Julio to her and her to him, we were not fooling Sin Corazón, manipulating her into feeling something that she would not ordinarily feel. We were presenting her and Julio with an opportunity that they could take or not. Do you understand, Little Wolf?"

"Yes, I think so," I said.

"For people of power in the world of sorcery, it is very difficult to make any kind of commitment. Now, Julio is a *curandero*—not a sorcerer, but he knows the world of sorcery. He has traversed those trails and knows them well, not that he has made them part of his life. Still in all, he is a man of power and has chosen to live with only a spirit mate."

"A spirit mate meaning like my spirit husband?" I said. "I just want to be sure I understand you."

"Yes, in other words if someone wanted to marry Julio, she would have to pay respects first to his spirit wife, who helps him in all of his healing endeavors. That is what she is there for—an adviser, as a helpmate, so to speak."

"This is confusing," I said.

"No," said Ruby, "only if you make it confusing. It is very, very simple."

"How is it simple, Ruby?"

"Well," Ruby said, twirling a long ringlet of her hair around her finger like a young girl and poking her other finger in her cheek. "It is simple, unless you want to make the world difficult, which you often do, Little Wolf. You challenge yourself by making things confusing, and then you work out the confusing aspects of your life little by little, adding tension and stress where they don't need to be."

"Oh, thank you, Ruby. I appreciate your sharing!" All the women laughed. "But really, I think it's important that I understand this completely."

"Yes, I think that's a good idea, too," Ruby said, making fun of me.

"Thank you, again, Ruby. Well, I am a person of power," I said.

"Ah, and is it difficult for you to make a commitment?" Agnes asked with a smile.

"Well, I suppose it is, but, but—"

"Well?" she said. "When you are a person of power, there is so much to you. Most people live in one tiny dimension of life. They put blinders on. They move forward. They are upstanding citizens, they make a good living, they work hard, they raise a family. But in the real truth of things, they don't see much. Not that they don't want to. It is their time in life. They're not quite ready yet to see all that is, and because of that, their lives are uncomplicated and they are perfect for mating. They can share a life very simply and they find someone who is also uncomplicated, and that's wonderful, too. This is not a judgment, just a fact."

"A person of power, like you, Lynn," Jaguar Woman said, "is looking for a very special person who is spiritual, a person who understands power, magical realms, dreaming. He doesn't have to be all that you are, but he must understand your power and respect it. Most important to you, I think, is respect. Somebody who knows who you are, who maybe doesn't follow you down all those trails. And I think that's what we're all looking for, no matter who we are in life. We need someone whom we can respect and who can respect us, even if our lives are vastly different. Sometimes that makes life very interesting."

"That's right," they said, laughing in unison.

"But a person of power like Julio has made a decision never to be a householder. Then he meets Sin Corazón, and he is in a tremendous internal war, trying to understand what he should do with his life. This will be a very interesting thing to watch because this is no ordinary man and certainly no ordinary woman. They have fallen in love in a way different from most other people in the world. Their suffering and joy will be profound because in their adjusting to each other, there will be tremendous pain. Do you understand that their worldview defines who they are? Their view of the world is built on freedom, which is very different from the point of view of someone who is married and committed in a love relationship."

"Yes," I nodded. "I would say so."

XXI

Jaguar Woman brought us together the next evening for a dinner of quesadillas, fresh papaya, and newly harvested corn. After a short siesta, we circled around, and Jaguar Woman, with great dignity and finesse, continued her storytelling.

Sin Corazón was sitting under a ceiba tree with her back against it, looking out across the fields of corn and the blue sky. She knew that the old sorcerer had tricked her one last time. She was ashamed of what she had tried to do with Lynn. A part of her wanted to die for the slip she had almost made. Maybe she could never really heal.

It was warm, but not uncomfortably hot. She was in so much emotional pain that she circled within herself like an animal looking for a safe place to spend the night. She knew that she had brought to herself this moment of loneliness and pain and abandonment. Again, she had betrayed a sister. She would not see Julio again, but the dream that they had shared seemed elusive, just out of reach. How could this be real or true? Her pain seemed complete. She heard the voice of Jaguar Woman inside her saying, "My daughter, there will come a time when you must hit bottom. You must go as deeply into your sorrow as you can go, and when that happens, sit with it. Sit inside of it. Wrap it around you. Cloak it over your face and your heart and your being. Don't move, don't try to run, don't try to change it. Don't try to do anything. This is not a moment for action. This is a moment simply to sit and find the end to the dark tunnel."

Sin Corazón followed those words because she did not
know what else to do. She could not reach out to anyone, and
it would not make any difference if she could. The distractions
were gone: love, the only hope she had felt, was being taken
from her.

So she sat and felt a gentle swirl of energy moving to the
right around her, as if she were again in the center of that
storm, as if somehow her stillness kept the outer perimeter
floating. In a sense she felt finally out of evil, out of love, out of
learning, out of apprenticeship, out of everything, as if there
was nothing left. Instead of sadness, she felt relief. There was
nothing left to try. She had learned and gathered much
throughout her lifetime; now if she did not let go of it forever,
it would destroy her. On the path to power and enlightenment,
there comes a time when you give up what you have accomplished, the mistakes you have made, and the goodness that
you have created. You don't own them anymore.

As she thought that, as she dreamt it, sitting there under
the ceiba tree, suddenly she realized that she was bleeding
profusely. She looked down at the ground, saw a red stain
moving out around her in the sand. As she stared in disbelief,
she began to see words in the blood, as if her own blood were
speaking to her. At first the language seemed confusing and
unfamiliar, and then she saw symbols that looked like people
and words that held music between the syllables—words
falling out of her as a gift to Mother Earth for all the wordless
wisdom that had been given to her from the mountains and
the valleys. She felt her body giving all of that wisdom back.
Flowing in the blood was her gratitude for life and all that she
had been given. Her body gave away to the body of Mother
Earth, as a mother sacrifices for the wholeness of her child. She
saw pictures of her own childhood and how she had sacrificed
for the mother she had never known. Was life all, in one way
or another, a blood sacrifice?

There was no reason for her to be bleeding. This was not the
time for her moon, but this moment of profound insight had

created a release in her spirit so that her body was also letting go. Then the tears came, and she cried. She cried for the bleeding of all women, for Julio, for the blood of life that has stained the earth since the beginning of humankind. She bled for the rhythms of life, for the rhythms of her own spirit. She bled for love and for what it had meant to her in her life. She realized that the blood was leaving her body, no longer with her, although she had created it. Love, she realized, is not separate from you. It is part of you. You're made of that love; there is no separation. The blood of your spirit is always the blood of your spirit. The blood of your body becomes the ashes of Mother Earth, becomes the death and the rebirth in the rebuilding.

As the pool of blood became larger, she realized that she was in danger of hemorrhaging to death. Her blood would nourish that ceiba tree. Am I pure essence? she thought. Instead, she leaned her back against the tree, even stronger, and thought that maybe this was the moment she had always been waiting for. In going toward life and living on the edge of life, always testing, always pushing the limits of endurance, pain, joy, maybe death was another mirror to be looked into and walked through. What was on the other side?

Then she heard the voice of Jaguar Woman. "Have you learned what you came here to learn?" she asked.

Sin Corazón thought for a long time.

"Do you still feel sad?" the voice asked. "Do you still feel pain?"

And Sin Corazón realized that the pain was still there, changed, different; that she had still not learned what she needed to learn about love. She knew she could live with it now. From this position in her life, she would not choose the dark side because of a banished love. She could allow herself to trust. That's what Jaguar Woman had meant: if she couldn't find trust, she could not have Julio.

She took a deep breath, shocked at her weakness, and chose life. She chose to go on, to find her way back home. Hours later Zoila helped her into the hut, giving her herbs to stop her bleeding. Sin Corazón fell asleep.

In the middle of the night she opened her eyes. She felt weak, exhausted, and full of joy at the same time, knowing that she had made the right decision. Standing in the doorway was a presence, which she realized was her teacher. Jaguar Woman stood there for a long time, the shadows so deep that Sin Corazón could not see her face. Jaguar Woman slowly walked across the room, lighting a candle and placing it next to the hammock where Sin Corazón lay.

Jaguar Woman sat on a painted red-and-blue chair and reached out to hold Sin Corazón's hand. Even Jaguar Woman was stunned at the weakness in her apprentice, who was usually so full of strength. To Sin Corazón, Jaguar Woman's hand felt like the paw of a giant cat—hard, padded, strong. Sin Corazón closed her eyes, pulling around her the stillness of the moment to give her strength and nourishment. She wanted nothing more than for this moment to continue.

"I love you," she said, her eyes still closed. "If only—"

"If only," Jaguar Woman interrupted, "we could learn by sitting here and holding each other's hands in perfect stillness, enjoying the bliss and the light and the shadows of life! You have paid your last debt."

"Yes," Sin Corazón said, understanding.

"You have come close to death, my daughter, and you chose well. You heard my voice?"

"Yes, and you answered my questions without my even having to ask them. What now?" Sin Corazón finally asked, not even really caring what the answer was. There had been too much, and now stillness was all she could bear.

A gentle wind came in from the door, bringing a scent of flowers that bloomed in the heat outside. Sin Corazón closed her eyes and passed into a deep sleep. She was not looking for dreaming, for answers, for anything but peace. All she wanted now was the acceptance that brings a kind of quietness and a comfort to the soul.

XXII

Julio's mind was besieged by shadows—unknown dark forms that approached in the night and made him sweat and ache in torment. They were not his allies, nor could he find their evil master. He was out of control—that state of being that he hated most. Despite all the ladders of light that he had created with Sin Corazón, now he blamed her. He needed to blame someone for his torment, needn't he? If this was love, he wanted no part of it! Sin Corazón's love and passion blinded him in reflection as he tore at his stomach and rolled around in the wilderness dirt, trying to hide or escape.

Clouds blew in—black, purple, clouds edged in gold and silver light. "No more will I see myself through the eyes of another," Julio vowed as he trudged up the trail winding beside a stream. For a moment he felt a presence near him. He looked up at the mountains, toward the rain that was certain to come, and felt his power shrinking inside him as he walked farther away from her. Lightning split the sky in golden shards of power. He hoped one would find him. "Rain, rain on me," he whispered as the thunder rolled over the mountains. "Wash away my madness and all my confusion."

The storm began to shake the earth. He sat on a flat stone and watched the stream whip into a fury. His blood pounded through his body, matching the tumultuousness of the flowing stream. Then the storm broke. The rain came in a torrent all around him but left him dry and untouched. It was then he realized that his pain was not enough rather than being too much. All the power and goodness of life, Sin Corazón and the exquisite softness of her body—none of it ever really had touched him, and he couldn't feel it deeply, ever. His loneliness was so profound that it filled him with hatred for those who could touch and feel and love. Could he cross this abyss and heal his longing and his terror?

"Where have you gone?" José asked his apprentice as he held Julio's face in his hands.

In a one-room hut in the mountains near San Cristóbal, José perused his apprentice with disgust.

The old man in a clean white tunic shirt, cotton pants, and sandals looked clean and crisp. His white hair was thick and cropped short. Julio sat on a wooden stool, with a sparse beard of a week or two, his hair wild and disheveled. His clothes were wrinkled and dirty. Julio could not look his teacher in the eye, he was so embarrassed. Nor could he seem to find his voice, so José found it for him.

"The two of you are playing a very dangerous game."

Julio nodded. "I can't function, I can't sleep, I'm going crazy," he muttered.

"I suppose you're even meeting allies of the devil?" José smiled.

"What do you mean?"

"Just as I thought." José nodded. His eyes snapped with light and color from the setting sun angling in through the window. "You better straighten this out right now, or those allies will be on your tail forever."

"But, but . . ." Julio began to shake.

"No damn buts about it. No apprentice of mine is going to get caught with his pants down like this."

With those words José ripped off Julio's pants, tore his dirty shirt to shreds, and, grabbing him by the back of his head, pushed the yelling Julio outside and into the stream that ran near the hut. José kept him facedown in the water until Julio was flailing and sputtering for air. Then José let go of him, and as Julio stood up he pushed him down again.

"What are you doing?" Julio screamed, completely furious.

"The same thing you're doing!"

"What does that mean?"

"You're drowning in the river of life. Sin Corazón is drowning every time you push her down. You're drowning from your own stupidity. Don't you see, you damn fool?"

"No, I don't see. And I'm not a fool."

"To me you look pretty foolish." José began to laugh.

"You're in love with someone who reflects you back to yourself, and you can't stand it. Sin Corazón saw her monsters that night by the fountain, and you helped her to heal. Now you have to let her heal you in the same way."

"But I can't do it. I don't want it," Julio whined.

José leapt up like the panther he is and struck Julio with his foot, sending him sprawling in the water. "Now, you hear me, Julio. This is big medicine for you. You asked this woman to *see* you, and she did. Now it's your turn. Don't you dare get heavy on me. You're taking an energy slave and that will not do. I will not have this kind of behavior. I do not respect it. You are forgetting everything you have learned. This bullshit could destroy your dreambody and more. Take hold of yourself. You both need this balance. It is perfect, and she's waiting for you. Remember who you are—quickly, before it's too late—and ask Sin Corazón to join with you in marriage."

After José left, Julio sat in solitude for several days. After nursing his injured ego, he felt as though a heavy crust of shell cracked and fell away. Inside was Julio's vulnerability, which he addressed for the first time in his life. For the first time he realized what he had wanted all along.

It took several days for him to convince Sin Corazón that his intentions were sincere. Then after a few days of being near each other, they both saw the growth that they had accomplished and how much they truly wanted to be together.

XXIII

Sin Corazón walked long and fast through the foothills around San Cristóbal. She knew that her deepest dream would soon be fulfilled, that she and Julio would finally join in a sacred wedding and they would work together as healers of the spirit and the body. She was concerned about Julio's ability to stay committed in such a relationship. He wanted this with his whole heart, as did she, but this was a new world for them both. There would be difficulty, and their life would not be a normal one in any sense of the word.

They had decided for the time being to go to Veracruz. Perhaps they would live there for a while. They had decided not to have children but to help people give birth to their own freedom and their acts of power. That would be children enough for them, for they did not wish to be tied down like José and Zoila. They wished to be free to enjoy their world of power and each other.

A stream had widened, forming a pool. Sin Corazón sat next to the water, underneath a tree struggling against the sun of the hot summer. I too must be a bit withered, she thought to herself. She felt an exhaustion deep inside herself, even as she was exhilarated at the prospects of her new life with Julio. She traced in her mind her incredible past. How could she have taken such a wrong turn so many years ago? The guilt had been erased, and what was left was a kind of silence and a deep sense of peace. She had been deeply immersed in both worlds—darkness and light; now, she knew, giving back to the universe all that she had taken would require a conscious effort full of her intent.

When a man or woman who was being seduced by the forces of evil came to her, Sin Corazón would know how to work to bring that person to a place of clarity and rebirth. She felt extraordinarily excited about that prospect. Looking out across the expanse of Mexico, she recalled teachers in ancient Mayan, Olmec, Toltec lifetimes. She recalled teachers in the sacred dreamtime and honored them, feeling the pain of centuries, of blood sacrifice and war. She thought about how darkness has prevailed upon the planet, has taken hold of people's lives and destroyed nations. Deep within her heart she felt the shadow and the light and the dance between the two: the tearing, the destruction. Everywhere around her was the crucible of transformation. It filled her, and she was made of it, and she understood it to the core of her being.

XXIV

Hand in hand, Julio and Sin Corazón stood at the edge of vast
Lake Atitlán in Guatemala. It was dusk, and as darkness
descended upon them, they continued to watch the reflection
of the stars and moon in the magnificent lake surrounded by
volcanoes.

The beautiful village of Panahachel lay nestled against the
shores and the cliffs to the south of the lake at the bottom of
the road from Solola. They sat on the beach and shared the
silence, listening to the lapping of the waves and looking at
the cliffs below Solola that rose hundreds of feet in the air.
They were waiting to see the fires of the shaman's caves,
which looked like stars fallen to Earth. As one was lit and
another and another, they knew that ceremony was beginning.

Julio was from one of the small villages along the lakeshore,
and he wanted to bring Sin Corazón to the world altar of stone
that had taught him so much about power in his early days of
training as a man of power. He wanted to share with her that
altar's power and its serenity.

A magical lake it was with the reflection of the silvery moon
and the mountain and the lights around it. It seemed to be
alive with a placid and yet giant power beneath the surface.
They would wait until morning to take a boat and cross the
short distance to his village. Lake Atitlán was treacherous, and
after four in the afternoon he knew better than to swim or take
a boat out into those waters. The volcano at the other end of
the lake from where they were sitting would sometimes create
small tsunami waves that had killed many people in the past.
Sin Corazón could feel the strength, as if a dragon were swim-

ming just out of sight, waiting to surface and let its strength be known.

Tomorrow they would be married. José and Zoila had come down for the ceremony. Jaguar Woman had not yet arrived, and they waited in anticipation of seeing her. This would not be an ordinary wedding but a marriage of agreement, a marriage of power between families of power. The Sisterhood would join in the festivities and the celebration. Julio and Sin Corazón were independent, eccentric, and unusual people who had treasured their aloneness in the world, their complete and total independence. So for both, the untamable power of Lake Atitlán mirrored an aspect of who they were in the world and an aspect of their magic.

Julio put his arm around Sin Corazón. His heart beat faster as he looked at her aquiline profile against the light of the moon. She was so beautiful to him. He could not believe that he was so lucky and fortunate that she loved him as much as he loved her. He placed his fingers under her chin and turned her eyes toward his.

"The lake water," he said, "is like our power."

"How do you mean?" Sin Corazón smiled at him.

"Water is like power, just as power is like water. It changes every day." He kissed her tenderly as they rose from the sand to walk into the village and spend their last night as a single man and woman.

14
The Reckoning

Striations of sunrise lighted the sky in an explosion of orange and purple. The old sorcerer sat on the top of the ancient Mayan Temple of the Sun. He was in a state of confusion and anger, fearing he might have lost Sin Corazón forever. He could not understand why his magic, which had never failed him once in all of his life, had gone wrong. That blond woman from the North had come very close to the gateway. But he knew that would have been a mistake.

He set out his talking crystals before him and watched the sun create prismatic reflections on the ancient stones around him. He read the signs, looking for something new that perhaps he had never seen before. Then it happened: a shadow from a bird in flight high above crossed his patterning in the sand and rubble and stone of the temple.

It was not a good premonition because the buzzards flew over from the left, moving toward the western gateway of death. Cold foreboding crawled up his spine. Again, he ran his fingers over his talking crystals, waiting for the words that always came to him but seemed to be failing him now. Then he looked into the rainbow gateway of his most powerful crystal, and for a moment saw the face of an older jaguar, not the young jaguar spirit of Sin Corazón. He gasped, realizing, of course, as he should have months before, that he was tangling with an ancient force that had been at war with him and his spirits since before Mayan times. He held the lines of human sacrifice between his teeth, like a horse taking hold of a bit. He had used those lines of sorcery and pain to control his apprentices. He recognized the face of Jaguar Woman. They had been opponents in many lifetimes, and, of course, it was she who was shielding him and his power from Sin Corazón. It was destiny, momentarily beyond his control. But he knew about his apprentice's need for excitement and power. The old sorcerer knew that if he could see her—hopefully unnoticed, which was his finest art—during a great moment of love like her wedding, then power could change in his favor, and he might still be able to pull Sin Corazón back.

He closed his eyes in an attempt to conjure a vision of her, working a long time before he saw her face. He searched for the lines of power on which to tug but found only empty space. Then suddenly out of an awesome radiance, he saw her eyes, filled with love and benevolence.

"Disgusting," he snarled to himself. "We'll see about this."

The old sorcerer was fired with the renewed energy of the ancient battle to steal power from those who possess light. More than even the lost apprentice, Sin Corazón, he wanted her light forever. In his mind, he would have it. Sooner or later he meant to have her back.

15

Dance of the cats

Wearing traditional Guatemalan huipeles and handwoven skirts, Agnes, Ruby, and I sat together with Zoila and José under a large rubber tree near the world altar overlooking Lake Atitlán. Evening was beautiful. The trees, filled with paper lanterns and lights, looked as if they were swarming with fireflies. The stone altar was covered with wrapped power bundles. Prayer sticks and candles, staffs, and many other things were set into the sand all around the altar and in the area nearby.

I kept looking for an old sorcerer with serrated teeth. My eyes could not see him, but I had a funny feeling that he was near. I was uneasy, and without Agnes's urging, I would not have come. I was still angry with Sin Corazón for trying to trick me. But everyone else was full of excitement and happiness. Not for a long, long time had we gotten together for such an occasion. I did my best to join in.

"Interesting," I whispered in Agnes's ear, "how Sin Corazón brings us together for very unusual occasions." Agnes laughed as we drank our lemonade.

The haze coming off the volcano was cool and comforting. Sin Corazón came over to us, carrying beautiful *milagro* necklaces she had made for each of us and placing them around our necks so they hung low over our chests. She kissed each of us on either cheek and thanked us very much for being there.

There were tears in her eyes as she held my hand and whispered to me. "I was so wrong that day. I will make it up to you. Forgive me once again, if you can."

Like everyone in the Sisterhood, I had made prayer sticks

for her, bound together to represent the female and the male in a state of bonding with prayers for their life together and continued happiness and power.

"Place them yourselves," Sin Corazón said, "on the altar as you see fit. I thank you, my sisters, for forgiving me. I am full." She placed her clenched fist over her heart and turned to rejoin Julio.

Julio seemed excited but completely in his center. That surprised me; I had expected him to be nervous, looking for an exit at every moment. Instead, he was obviously very settled and secure with his decision. He constantly had his eye on Sin Corazón, not jealously but watching to see if she needed support or help in any way.

I took a deep breath, as did Agnes and Ruby. The couple's happiness together was a moment to be shared and to behold, a moment of joy. Then the drumming began. Several of the young men from the surrounding villages began to play flutes. There were people at this gathering whom I had never seen. I knew that two young men were from Peru and one was from Chile, and they joined in the festivities, playing lilting music that got everyone into a mood of celebration.

Then Julio and Sin Corazón approached the altar together. Jaguar Woman joined them, as did José and Zoila. Julio and Sin Corazón made vows to each other, asking for guidance on their respective paths of power, and they gave each other gifts for their medicine bags. Crystals were exchanged and shaman stones with rings around them. They exchanged objects wrapped in natural red material; only they knew the contents.

This was a wedding like none I had ever seen, outside under power trees, in front of a world altar that brought together the history of shamanism and *curanderos* the world over. On that altar people of power from all around the globe were represented. It was magnificent to share the uniting of forces in a gathering of simplicity, with baskets and clay pots of melon and salads and food of every kind. There was a softness in the air, a sense of support.

I thought back on the extraordinary trail that had led these two people to this moment, and I honored them from my heart, knowing what an extraordinary struggle they had both been through. It was a wonder, really, in a sense, that they were even alive. I wondered what kind of karma Sin Corazón would face in this life because of the pain she had inflicted on others. Was she done with those decisions? Were they done with her? Negativity had come to pass only within moments of terror in Sin Corazón's heart, but in reality she had even surmounted the fears of retribution that Jaguar Woman had told her about and transformed them into this incredible moment of happiness.

"Sin Corazón is a very powerful woman," I whispered to Ruby.

"Yes, my daughter, she is something."

Her long black hair flowed down to her waist. Soon it would be worn in braids. What a beautiful woman! we all thought.

"And what a dangerous woman she is," Ruby said, winking with her blind eye.

"Yes," I nodded, wondering if I could completely forgive her.

The darkness became inky blue. Purple shadows elongated across the lake and the clearing around us. Sin Corazón and Julio began to dance together at the end of the ceremony. Jaguar Woman walked into the middle of the dancing couples, holding something high in her left hand, and stopped before Julio and Sin Corazón.

"This is a gift to you. Actually, Sin Corazón, I believe it belongs to you. We both know, you and I, the depths of the pain and wisdom that you have brought to people in this world, to me and to your sisters. It is no secret what you have lived through, the choices you have made, the paths you have chosen through these many years. In forgiveness is creativity, and in love we are reborn. So my apprentice, my daughter, I give to you this garnet that has always been meant for you. It is your shaman's jewel."

At the mention of those last two words, gasps rose here and there in the Sisterhood. Was there to be some kind of a confrontation? But there was none. Jaguar Woman was speaking with love from her heart, not with anger. In her presence, all was well.

I remembered back to our dreaming together, the four of us, Agnes, Ruby, and Jaguar Woman. I remembered Julio coming up in that dream, and Jaguar Woman sharing her thoughts on transformation through love and partnership: it had come to pass. Sin Corazón owed a great deal to her teacher for this moment of blessing.

Jaguar Woman placed the garnet sphere into Sin Corazón's hand. Sin Corazón accepted the return of her most sacred object. Tears splashing down her cheeks, she hugged her teacher. Then Jaguar Woman, blessing her and Julio with her macaw feather fan, turned and, leaving the ceremony, disappeared into the darkness.

As Jaguar Woman disappeared from view, I heard a rustling in the leaves off to the left on the trail. For a moment I thought I saw the old man's face shining in the moonlight, salt-and-pepper hair curling around his face in a thick frame for the piercing eyes. Then he was gone. I felt a chill. Had I been seeing things, or was the old sorcerer watching his apprentice sever all ties with him forever? Agnes put her arm around my shoulder. "He's gone for now." Then she had seen him too! "There's too much power here, but he will return one day."

"Will he try to take her?"

"I am sure of it," she said. "But let it go. The moment is beautiful, and we must not ruin it. If he comes, he comes. She will have to face her past one more time, and trust in her power."

Later that night, we walked back to the village down by the shore of Lake Atitlán. I heard a heavy crushing high in the branches in the tree next to me. It looked like a rubber tree with orchids winding through the branches, beautiful in the moonlight. Then there came another crash of branches cracking and brushing against one another.

We looked up into the tree. Silhouetted against the moon was a huge female jaguar leaping from one branch to another. She was followed by a black panther, sleek, equally large, leaping from branch to branch and tree to tree.

It was an awesome sight. We sat down on the trail where we stood, wanting not to be seen, to observe these extraordinary cats.

"Do panthers and jaguars play together?" I whispered to Ruby and Agnes, their heads close to me. Agnes's eyes shone in fascination.

The cats reached a tree together, each swaying on separate branches. They pawed each other, licking each other as if they were mates. Then it dawned on me. "Agnes, what is Julio's power animal?"

"What do you think?" she answered.

The young female jaguar reached out her paw and caressed the black panther. The black panther hollowed its spine with pleasure, and the jaguar bared her claws ever so slightly. The panther reached around, baring his fangs, and nipped her on the neck gently, affectionately. Then the jaguar lengthened her claws even more. This time, the black panther reached its head around and nipped more seriously. The two of them reared back on their haunches, pawed each other almost to the point of fighting. The jaguar leapt away under the branches of another tree. For a moment they were invisible as they swayed and flung leaves and vines into the darkness surrounding them. Only the sounds of their heavy bodies and the low throaty whines and growls of two giant cats, predators of the rain forest, could be heard on the damp evening air.

And so it is that they play. So it is that they love and toy with each other, testing each other's strengths and abilities to the edges of life and death. This was no ordinary mating, but a mating of love and of one kind of power. Mated for life, they would fight to the death for each other without a thought for their own demise. They were two powerful predators standing alone within the vastness of their own universe, within the circle of their own caring. Often their power shields would set one upon the other, but only for a moment, like the jaguar's claws sinking more deeply into the black panther. It was only allowed momentarily before a warning was given. And so they live.

16

Love and Wisdom

Through Jaguar Woman's skill and beauty as Storyteller, she had entranced all of us. Because of the struggle for love and truth between Sin Corazón and Julio, I didn't want the story to end. And, of course, it goes on. But for now the artifice of Jaguar Woman's fluid voice, her movements and relentless pace and timing were ended. I had learned so much. To assimilate all that had transpired, I needed to walk in the wilderness with the memory of her words.

That evening on our return to her village in Mexico, we feasted together and celebrated Jaguar Woman, the Twisted Hair.

A day later, Jaguar Woman and I were walking down a trail near Palenque.

"It was important for you to hear the story of Sin Corazón and Julio as I spoke of it."

"Why is that?" I asked. "What does that have to do with the clay pots?" I asked.

"Because the clay pots and their information must be assimilated in a special way."

"I don't understand," I said.

"To understand the message of the clay pots, you must have an ability within you to open up your heart to such a degree that you become full of light." Jaguar Woman spoke in a halting way, as if trying to find words to express what she really meant. "And when I say light, Black Wolf, I hesitate even to describe the faculty needed to understand what is in the clay pots. You do not assimilate the information as you would if you were a student in a university. It isn't the words or what the words are saying, it's the wisdom between the words that's so very important. The clay pots are never revealed to anyone who would look at them as an anthropologist. The knowledge is shamanic, from the energy sources in the universe. I am speaking of love, the aspect of love in the sense of the Great Spirit—Godness."

I was sitting in the shade of a large-leaf tree with orchids growing in its branches all the way up to the top. It was like being in my own private botanical garden, magnificently wild and tangled and rich in flowers and various kinds of plants.

"Is that why you spoke of light?" I asked.

"Yes, Black Wolf. Light, meaning the ability to bring a kind of radiance into your own being and also project it into the world. That is a tall order, for anyone. You are ready to read the contents of the first pot, or so Agnes told me. That is very exciting indeed. As we work together in the coming years, all of the pots will be revealed to you, one by one. You will take that knowledge, as it is appropriate, to your people."

"So the relationship of Sin Corazón and Julio—"

"It was important for you to understand the dark and the light side of love. Not that you didn't understand much of this already, but the relationship between Julio and Sin Corazón is a powerful example of evil being transformed through love."

"Yes," I said, "I'm fascinated to see how they lead their life together, both of them being solitary beings in so many ways."

"It is a relationship of power," she said. "It truly was a sorcerer's wedding in many ways. And through their story you grew tremendously. Because of that, you are now ready for the wisdom of the seven clay pots. Soon you will journey back to the cave with Agnes. Our experience together here in the Yucatán has been a great gift to all of us, and I love you, my daughter."

"And I love and honor you," I said.

Jaguar Woman hugged me and pulled me up by the hand. "Come. Dinner will soon be ready, and it is important that you get a long sleep tonight so that you can leave very early in the morning and still be rested. You have quite a journey of discovery ahead of you."

The sun was setting as we walked back down the trail toward her village. Long tree shadows marked our trail as we walked close together, full of love and respect for each other.

17
The Secret Prophecies
of the Clay Pots

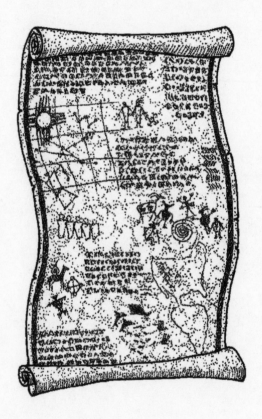

After a long journey home and a few days of resting and long walks, Agnes and I returned to the cave of the seven clay pots. Entering the magnificent cavern, we spent a long time performing the appropriate ceremonies.

I was so excited that all I wanted to do was begin. I didn't care about my aching body or my moments of claustrophobia inside the cave. Carefully, I set out the scroll, with stones holding the corners, Agnes helping me. I took out my papers and my pen and began to work.

I ran my fingers gently over the scroll, honoring it. The letters of each word were raised slightly from the surface of the scroll itself. I read the first part of the information, which was about why we are here on this earth and where this knowledge has come from. I looked over at Agnes, who was equally as excited by my own anticipation for what was before me.

"Agnes, this is saying that this knowledge was carefully placed on this earth many, many thousands of years ago. There have been many periods of recorded history—some we know of, like Atlantis and Lemuria, and many that have been long forgotten and buried."

"Yes," Agnes said, and pointed to one of the many designs that intersected the sentences. On either side of a drawn line there were indications of people, shields, and heads severed from their bodies. "Because of a great war, the knowledge that had been given readily to everyone interested in knowledge and evolving toward God suddenly was shut down. Many of the good people here on this planet, knowing full well that the

Earth is a schoolhouse, were destroyed. Because of that, the sacred keepers of this knowledge became women, who were hidden along with their children. These warring factions were after the warriors; it was they who were killed. So the women—the keepers of the knowledge from forty-four power points around the earth—developed what you might call certain environmentally based technologies beyond even what we know now.

"Consider this paper," she said, holding it very carefully and gently between her fingers. "This was created thousands and thousands of years ago. It's like new because it was treated with herbal formulas that have long been lost. The ancient Egyptians knew of these formulas for mummification, for instance. The Mayans knew of these formulas—some of them."

"Now, Agnes, it says here—help me understand this. There was an arrow and there were mountains, and then it looks like plains here. Is that correct?"

"Yes. Actually this is desert," she said.

"Does this point mean south . . . ?

Agnes interrupted me. "This circle here with these dots represents the body of what is now called North America, the United States. And this here is part of Canada," she said. "These circles and these dots represent ceremonies that were done. As you see, this symbol represents the sun and this over here represents the moon. Essentially, these were male ceremonies and female ceremonies. But down here," she said, pointing to the end of the scroll, "represents what is now Mexico and the sacred Mayan lands.

"Remember the seven cities of gold or Cibola? That was a story used to trick the conquistadors. It was not a total lie, actually, because there was such a place—a sacred place. But the gold was the knowledge, the wisdom, that was held here. That is to the south, and that is another teaching. Much of the knowledge comes from what sometimes are called the zero chiefs, the sacred count. Many of the sacred wheels are not only Native American, but they also come from an older history, from way before the Toltecs. That knowledge was preserved in the seven sacred cities.

"This cave is an energy line between those seven sacred cities. That knowledge and wisdom touch the seven pots' knowledge and wisdom and are held within the hand of the seven stars. It is from the seven stars that this knowledge came. So as you open this pot, you pick up an energy line that will be secured on a psychic level into your solar plexus. It will help you and give you strength in your dreaming. It will eable your dreambody to go beyond what it has known before. You will have knowledge, but you won't know where it came from. The bridge is the Sisterhood, and for you, we are the beginning of your journey back home."

"But Agnes, I have always thought that you were my home, that I lived in your heart and in the heart center of the Sisterhood."

"Yes, my daughter, but all of us come from somewhere else."

I looked at her with deep appreciation and admiration, and then returned to the scroll and began to write more of what lay before me. To my surprise, the next section had to do with how we recognize ourselves as beings of light who were sent here to grow and to learn, choosing the physical body to be our sacred lodge, and how that sacred body provides a mirror. All of these teachings the Sisterhood already had imparted to me, as I have imparted in my books and have been teaching to my apprentices. But this was the first time that I had known the source of that knowledge. I am paraphrasing this translation. As I read each sentence, Agnes would help me to decipher or make clear what was found there. A few sentences later, the scroll described recognition—that we would recognize one another through our eyes. Those of us who are feeling isolated, feeling adrift on a vast expanse of lonely consciousness, yet understanding many things that others seem blind to, would find one another. We are children of an awesome force, and our test is to find our way through this wilderness, strange and unknown to us in many ways. Out test is to locate our sisters and brothers and support them. Our first lesson is to understand that we are here to learn, here to find our way back to the Godness that we are.

"Agnes, I've always meant to ask you this, but why do we have to go through so much pain? Yes, to grow you need to move through the crucible of fire. I understand that! But if we have been home once, why didn't we just stay there?"

Agnes found this hilarious and laughed as she always does when I have made a seemingly stupid comment. But I made her answer me.

"My daughter, we can never explain the mysteries of the Great Spirit. Why does power work in the way it does? This is not for me to explain or even to bother myself with. All I'm concerned about is what *is*. There is no 'normal life' or explaining the 'challenge of life.' There is only life."

"Agnes, you must know more than you're telling me!"

"Of course I know more than I'm telling you! If I took this experience away from you, it would be lost to you forever. You have to grope around in the darkness, skin your knees, bump your head, and break your heart over and over again until you learn. But when you do learn, my daughter, you will have learned *forever*.

"Do you think I did not ask these questions before I found the answer? Do you think any of the great teachers have not asked the same questions? Because of your yearning to know, because of your curiosity and innocence and your own sense and relationship with power, you can keep going even when so many forces in the world try to destroy you. Of course they're trying to destroy you, because they're an opposite force. Their negativity and ignorance want to survive as much as you do."

"But if I learn and understand and become wise, that doesn't mean that all else cannot coexist with me."

"Oh?" Agnes responded. "When your light becomes greater,

then darkness disappears. How can there be darkness when the sun is shining? It simply cannot happen. They know that, and they want to diminish your light every day and on every step of the way along your path."

"But Agnes," I said, going back to my original question, "how is it that we could have left home in the first place?"

"Sometimes, Little Wolf, you don't realize that you're home. You don't realize what you have until you lose it. It's one of the greatest lessons of any lifetime on the path of spirit."

The scroll went on to say that when you are incarnated onto this earth, you are filled with possibility for cellular rejuvenation. You are given the possibilities, in other words, to live on this planet for as long as you would like. But it is up to you to find those possibilities. One of the big lessons of the scroll, it seemed to me as I copied it carefully, was to find these possibilities—to awaken them by opening your heart to the vibrations of light, although *vibrations* was not the word used.

The scroll described using the power of the mind—which I interpreted as visualization and dreaming—to fill your blood cells with light. What you imagine can be real. The reason we age, it said, is because certain cells (super T cells, I believe) lie dormant within our bodies, and we don't know how to awaken them. Cellular light activates them. Once they are functioning, we will have no more disease as we know it. This was all described with words, lines like lightning flashes, and a tiny sun radiating within a goddess-like figure of fecundity.

There were different symbols for the heart—the heart within trees, within mountains, within water places. There were pictures of children, meaning, as I understood it, for us to approach the world with total openness and a heart full of innocence, from a place of nonjudgmental peace. The definitions I found had a lot to do with beauty: in beauty is truth.

The scroll went on to say that this lifetime was a great gift to any soul, that the possibility of enlightenment was within reach of any of us in any lifetime if we chose. We are here to learn, wake up, and find the essence of one's spirit—remember who we are. This was said in many different ways. We would recognize one another by the fact that we would feel lonely on our paths, isolated from others in so many ways. So much that happens in our world would feel alien to us. Because we feel special in some way and because of our almost artistic approach to the world, we would find our way difficult. That is by design: it's what we have chosen, what must be. The scroll intimated that only through the trials of a challenged life would we grow into a state of perfection.

As I wrote and wrote, my heart began to expand. Going through this experience made me feel extraordinarily blessed and gifted by spirit. I wondered at the darkness in the world today, at the extraordinary difficulty that people of spirit are experiencing. How fortunate I am to have my teachers, to be able to bring this knowledge to others, to write books, to practice and be teaching.

From time to time, Agnes would ask me to stop. She would give me water. She had brought bananas and plums and a couple of pieces of beef jerky to help get me through the long night ahead. This time we could stay the night, Agnes told me, because now I was allowed to read the contents of the first pot.

"Why has it taken society so long to become open to these ideas, where it's even possible for authors to speak or to write of their findings?"

"Because we lost our way under a great wave of evil. It is pictured there"—she pointed—"the dark forces that moved onto this planet have sidetracked our energies so often. So much has had to remain hidden. There is no question that power is shifting. Just as they predicted that the poles will shift in the near future, so will the balance of power."

The scroll said that we are in an intense war against evil now, and that the evil is disguised. What we need is balance and awareness.

The drawings around the margins of the scroll went seemingly backward. Instead of starting at the left and working around sunwise, they started at the right and worked around differently on a page from how I expected. There was a lineage of stars, then what looked like meteors falling to the earth and to other planets, although I did not know which planets they were. Then there was a different geography off the coast of California. There were islands, much bigger and longer, where the Hawaiian Islands are now. Other land masses were connected. Either these drawings were of predicted changes or were records of how the earth appeared before the writing of this scroll.

Other drawings predicted fires, floods, earthquakes, and what looked like earth changes that moved according to the spiritual health of the planet. It stated that first is spirit, second is physicalness within the world of manifestation. As we grow in a spiritually healthy way, the earth will be healthy also. There were even drawings of hundreds of trees being cut in the south of the maps, which to me seemed like the rain forests. I don't think I missed much. I needed to move through this carefully.

Agnes quizzed me on many things. As always, she made the translation and the writing of the scroll part exercise and part learning. She would point to figures drawn and ask me to look at them. Then she would make me turn away from the scroll and ask me to describe exactly what I had been looking at. I found that in my excitement, I was missing things, such as the number of lines or configurations of the sun or the moon or the stars. She did this over and over again until my intent and my attention were acutely clear.

Again I traced my fingers gently across the scroll. The lettering was raised in one place where a kind of map had been drawn. I could see it described a fork in a trail. It spoke about a particular time in history when we would have a choice, not unlike the Hopi prophecies that humanity could save the world by choosing a balanced life of spirit. But if we choose an absence of spirit and a life of only materialism and greed, then not only will we fail but Mother Earth, too, will falter and die. This particular section spoke again about the seven stars, that all of the holiness that had ever been on the earth was from the Pleiades. Each of the religions that had thrived on this planet came from one or the other of the seven stars.

The scroll also spoke about the important mirror that materialism provides within the physical world. If we miss that lesson, we miss understanding why we were born onto a physical planet. Out of materialism comes a kind of striving that can destroy you: to become lost in the darkness of power without spirit is to be lost forever.

The last line was very clear. It said, "Only through love can you heal the evil that threatens to overtake you as a people."

By the time I finished copying the scroll, my eyes hurt and my back ached. I was completely exhausted. Agnes and I lay down on the floor in a specific position with our bodies aligned to the Pleiades, as positioned in the universe on the ceiling of the cave. Agnes asked me to shut my eyes, move into a state of dreaming, and allow myself to call in the keeper of the seven clay pots. "Remember carefully the messages that were given to you."

I moved my position, with my head pointing toward the sun and my feet toward the moon painted in flares of mica. Again I closed my eyes, and almost immediately my head began to throb. A tremendous amount of energy was coursing through my body. For a moment it was so strong I thought that I would surely be sick to my stomach.

Agnes placed her hand on my solar plexus, and with a very gentle pressure she reminded me to breathe. Sensing that I was having trouble, she got up, rested my head in her lap, and she placed her hands over my ears for several minutes. Then she ran her thumbs behind my ears, pressing hard into my muscles and down to my skull.

As she did so, the cavern began to spin. I kept my eyes closed, knowing that if I could simply concentrate and hold my center of power, the spinning would cease. Suddenly, my dreambody moved out through the top of my head. I found myself floating around up toward the ceiling, thinking that I needed to stay within the cavern. Below me I saw my body, Agnes still holding my head, her eyes closed in prayer. Then, not really thinking about what I was doing, my dreambody simply moved up through the narrow air shaft.

Suddenly in front of me was a great dreaming bear. She was an enormous grizzly, standing with her front paws lifted toward the sky. She turned around, showing me four sides of herself, as a power animal would do. Then, again facing me, she sat down and began to open her chest and her belly with her giant claws. There was no blood, no apparent showing of pain, almost as if she were opening an overcoat. Inside her sat a very old woman of unknown culture. She was light of skin, and her long, dark hair, streaked with gray, hung all the way to the floor. She looked at me with glowing curiosity. I looked back at her. It was not an uncomfortable stare, simply an exchange of love and an understanding that somehow we knew each other from long ago. I had hundreds of questions for her, but I was so in awe and spellbound that I simply sat there, trembling in my dream-body, aching to understand more. She smiled gently, as a mother would smile at her child. I sensed that she knew everything that I was feeling and thinking.

All she said was, "Seven clay pots." She reached out her left hand to me—her hand of power—and I clasped it with my left hand of power. I sensed an unfamiliar kind of energy field; her touch seemed to change me in some way.

"Teach me, Grandmother," I finally stammered. "I honor you with my life."

The old wise one nodded, and she stood up. The bear—obviously her totem—seemed to be standing behind her, protecting her and standing guard as the old woman approached me. She put her hands on the top of my head, then slowly ran her hands over my entire body. As she did so, my dreaming skin fell away like a suit of clothing, as the bear had fallen away from her. I stood before her, naked in my dream bones, afraid to move. For a moment I wondered if my skin would ever come back. I reminded myself that this was my dream-body. She turned me around four times, then she simply stepped back to her seat.

"Now," she said, "you are beginning to change." I looked at her with a question in my eyes. "When the seven pots are presented to you and you know of their position on this earth, when you begin to learn of the greater meanings of life—when your heart is open, because only in your innocence can you find me—then the spirit of the seven clay pots enters you. And you become pregnant with knowledge you did not know that you had. In becoming the mother of wisdom, your body begins to change slowly, but definitely. The wise among you will look at you and know you are different. To the rest of your people, you will appear to be the same. But nothing is the same forever. That is the gift of the seven clay pots: they give you the meaning for why you are here."

She took my hands and held them to her forehead and then to her heart. As she did so, my dreambody became complete again. It looked the same, but it felt different somehow.

"We will see each other again" were her final words. She disappeared inside the body of the great dreaming bear, who now became ferocious and threatening, and advanced toward me very aggressively.

Suddenly I was back in my body. Agnes awakened me. "You've been unconscious for several hours," she said. "It is time. We always have to leave the cave at a given hour. It is essential, and it is law."

She showed me how to do the appropriate ceremony, how to roll up the scroll in the proper way with blessing and with care. I did so as carefully as I knew how. Then we prayed together, traversing the universe on the floor, leaving offerings, and finally placed the clay pot back on the shelf next to the others. How I wanted to touch the others; I wanted to read their contents, but I dared not. I remembered how the Shaman's Jewel was pictured in the scroll. It was even prophesied that it would be threatened, that its ceremonial presence must be kept secret among the forty-four women who protected it.

Slowly we left the cavern and wound our way back up to the entrance. Again, it surprised me how easily the great stone rolled back into place. Then with branches of chaparral we swept the ground impeccably so that no one who passed this way—which would be very surprising—could ever tell another human had been on this trail.

We proceeded back down the precipitous path, through the foothills toward Agnes's cabin. Agnes asked me to be silent and walk quietly, thinking about all I had learned, about the place we all have within this universe of mystery.

The sun slid beneath the horizon. It was a long night of spirit and a night of tender thoughts of the grizzly and the old woman, the keeper of the seven clay pots.

18
The Wheel of the Dark Sister

Agnes and I were eating at the wooden table in Agnes's cabin.

"Agnes, this has been the first time I have written about our life together through a third person. Weaving all of this together has been one of the greatest challenges I have had to face—to pull all of the pieces together, to dream Sin Corazón, to be afraid of getting involved with her in any way, and yet, writing her story so that other people can gain knowledge and wisdom from all of the challenges she faced. I wondered, How will I ever string these events all together so they make sense? There's so much I've wanted to say that maybe did not fit into the story at the moment—perhaps I can mention them at another time, depending on when you want certain aspects of this knowledge revealed."

"Well," said Ruby, walking out of the shadows where she had been, presumably resting, "I think you've been doing a capital job. The allure of this discussion no longer serves me. See you in the morning."

Agnes and I stared at each other in surprise at Ruby's abrupt behavior. Shrugging our shoulders, we gave each other a hug and prepared for sleep.

As we slipped into our sleeping bags, I heard Agnes clear her throat. "Little Wolf," she said in a sleepy voice, "what really made it so difficult for you?"

"I think it is the fact that I have been almost a Pollyanna about working in the light. I didn't even want to explore thoughts or acts of evil. The dark side seemed part of a world of pain and treachery that I wasn't interested in. Yet I always knew it was something that I needed to understand. Otherwise, how could I guide someone who was lost in those dimensions?"

"That is correct, Lynn. More than that, you needed to understand the struggle and seduction of a truly dark sorcerer. What they do often looks like something attractive, even though it is not. Or so often, manipulators take you in and make you become a part of their lives, always make you feel that if anything's wrong, it's your fault, not theirs. In that guilt lies the beginning of their power."

The next day, the three of us sat under the poplar trees, mending our ceremonial items.

"Did Red Dog have anything to do with the extraordinary journey of Sin Corazón?" I asked.

Ruby set the moccasin that she was beading into her lap and looked my way. Her face with its high cheekbones was as familiar to me as my own. When I had occasion to touch her cheek, her weathered, beautiful, tan skin was like velvet.

"Red Dog was your first true lesson from the dark side, Little Wolf. Red Dog embodied the sorcerer, the man who used women's power and their sexuality. He made their dreams his own, captured them literally for his own manipulation."

"So in her dark days," I said, "Sin Corazón was the feminine reflection of Red Dog. Would you agree?"

"You could say that," Ruby said. "With Red Dog around, you were careful how you lived because you knew he might test you at any moment. Certainly you never saw him until the latter moments of a confrontation. But you could feel him tapping you, even when you least expected it. So you would feel that needling. It was sort of like this," she added, tapping the tip of her finger against her needle. "Maybe it wouldn't break the skin of your consciousness, but you felt it on the periphery of your knowing. You waited, and you became alert. Sin Corazón was the same way. Like all people who move around the sacred wheel of sorcery and darkness, they are caught within their own weakness in all four directions."

I smiled to myself: hugging Ruby was sort of like hugging a rosebush—I did so carefully, so as not to be punctured by a mood swing or a painful lesson.

Agnes began to smooth the ground between us. She drew a circle, then drew a cross in the center of that circle, marking the four directions.

"South," Agnes put in, "on the wheel of darkness is greed— for physical things, for the manifestation of ideas into the physical through unworthy manipulation and accumulation through theft and, often, abuse.

"West is envying other people's dreams and wanting to take what other people have accomplished. That's why southwest is the place of the dark sorcerers because they are always stuck between envy and greed. So often, they absolutely believe that they *own* the truth, that they own ideas. They may give lip service to the Great Spirit, but within their hearts, they claim all the credit. Then they lose that energy line to the Great Spirit— it is gone!

"In the north of the wheel of darkness is what other teachers have called a kind of spiritual materialism. It is using spirit falsely. This is an important position to understand. In the old days, people of spirit were cared for by the community and by the Great Spirit. But they lived in a much smaller world, where the demands of material life were almost nonexistent. Today it's a challenge for people to balance monetary needs with the world of spirit. It's one of the lessons we've come to learn here in an overpopulated society, and it must be understood carefully.

"On the wheel of darkness the position of spirit is idolatry. In truth, no one stands between you and your god. Sacredness comes only when you have made your acts of power and disappeared into them. It is then the Great Spirit sheds light into your being and all around you, and you begin to walk your true path. Also, in the north in spirit is the fixation of ideals, the inability to grow, rigidity of perception so that you no longer see the oneness of life but only your own limited position within it.

"In the east of the wheel is the position of the untrue mind—in other words, the need for manipulation and control and jealousy. This position is very powerful because people who live within it need to control everything around them—but only for their own good. Not for the good of the Great Spirit, or for what's right and best for the world. It's only one's own private gain, at all costs.

"And yes, a dark sorcerer's abilities move around this wheel. In the beginning, Sin Corazón moved into a position of learning and curiosity. There's a difference between curiosity and innocence. When you are curious, oftentimes you are cunning: you take what isn't yours, and you never trade for what you get. That begins the path of darkness. Sin Corazón moved into the jungles; she studied with that great sorcerer, and learned much. Remember, he will come after her, try to hurt her, and destroy this relationship between her and Julio, because he wants to keep her for his own—from his position in the east.

"So in the beginning, Sin Corazón moved with him into the sorcerer's wheel. She learned the physical knowledge of stalking, manipulation, and evil ceremony. Then she moved up to the north in spirit, but his stagnant ideals limited her vision of what truth is. But through his power and the focus he takes, she was able to glean much. She is talented and can learn quickly because of what the Sisterhood already taught her. She was able to create a bridge between darkness and light, and walk that bridge without being seen at first.

"Told that her husband had left with another woman, she moved to the west. The process of grief brought her to her knees. Her sacred dream fled from the shock. Not until now, through her relationship with Julio, was she able to bring that dream back into her heart. She moved into the dark west of the evil dream where death is close. She used death as an ally because she was unafraid; she could have died at any time after she lost her husband. She really thought she had no reason to live, except for the dark aberrations of power that she enjoyed from time to time.

"In the east she became a master of control, and she controlled through men, giving nothing in return. She brought no light into anyone's life, even her own."

Agnes paused for a moment and frowned.

"Little Wolf, what is the one thing she lost sight of and has now regained? What is it that a dark sorcerer loses in this process? She knew how to trick in every way, how to conceal without being seen, and how to conjure the darkest dream and manifest it into life."

"I can't imagine that kind of power," I said.

Ruby giggled at me and shook her head.

"You see," I said, "I have always been in awe of Sin Corazón. Not afraid of her, because I don't believe in what she does. But also I find that a sorcerer never kills you, she makes you kill yourself with your own terror."

Ruby agreed, as did Agnes.

"But what I see missing in both Red Dog and Sin Corazón at her darkest is creativity. Why is that?"

"Because," Agnes said, "she was so present in her darkness."

I thought about that for some time, and then I realized what she was saying.

"You mean she was so present in her focus to be evil that her ego became enormous."

"Yes," Agnes said, "and when you create such a monstrous ego, what happens? Look all around you and your society. You don't have to be wandering the hills and the wilderness. What about the sorcerers on Wall Street? What about the sorcerers who call themselves lawyers and doctors and politicians? Not that there aren't many good lawyers and doctors, but many do not come from the heart and a place of healing. What about them?"

"In people like that, I see a lack of inspiration." I looked at the wheel in the sand in front of me and pointed to each of the positions. "When a person is full of envy, they can't be creative or be inspired. They can only stand in their own way, creating shadows of their own misery. Then you move to the east. How can someone who has an untrue mind ever give birth to a new idea? So there can be no beauty in darkness, because in beauty is creativity."

We continued to work on our sashes and moccasins. Suddenly, I put down my work.

"The emptiness and the loneliness must be beyond comprehension," I finally said. "I cannot imagine how painful it must be to be that alone. In the east on this wheel, there's no way you can communicate because your need to control is so profound that you cannot ever put yourself forward and be close to someone. Only in a situation you can control completely would you feel safe enough even to give an opinion."

"Ah," Agnes said, "but it is a road of separateness by choice. These people have apprentices from time to time, but they touch them very lightly. Everything is about focus and personal power, so that they can do their chosen manifestations of evil. These people choose loneliness because of their own greed and envy, which they feed off of. It's what gives them the strength to go on. It is not a good place to be, but each of us needs to know what it means to be lost in greed or envy. Steer clear of those people unless you have true facility and understanding of how to heal them—and they have to want that healing. For the most part, they will hate you and will do everything possible to put out your light."

I took a deep breath and looked up at the mountains surrounding us. There were deep creases of dark green, purple, and indigo shadow as the sun moved lower in the sky. The cottonwoods, poplars, and elms down by the river were quaking in the gentle breeze. I watched the mountains as the shadows became deeper, preparing themselves for the night. How much of life—stalking and the hunting and the pursuit of survival—lives only during the darkness? I wondered. In all of us, some wildness is left unexpressed.

"Our way of arranging rules and commitments keeps so many of us from ever experiencing that wild spirit in all of us," I told my teachers. "When that becomes distorted—as it does, say, when Death Mother or Crazy Woman is not expressed—she moves into the night, doesn't she? She moves into places that are secret, unseen, and forbidden simply to live, simply to survive. If only we could have celebrations where we could express all aspects of our being, the darkness would not encroach into the very essence of our being and distort our way of loving and thinking."

"But that is why you write, my daughter. That is why we are here on this earth—to give away what has been gifted to us so that we may paint a reflection of the Great Spirit into everyone who wants that love to reside within them."

"Creativity has been always a process of spirit for me," I told Agnes. "When I've felt closest to you, when I have felt actually closest to the Great Spirit, then I move into a place of bliss—the only word to describe the feelings that well up within me."

Ruby got up, dusted herself off with her hands, and began to walk around me, scuffing her feet, making plenty of noise.

"Ruby, what are you up to?"

"Why would I be up to anything?" Ruby asked. "Is that a nice way to talk to an old Indian woman who needs to stretch her legs? Just because you young ones never get stiff doesn't mean that I can't get up and walk around if I feel like it!"

The sun was completely down now. It was a warm night, and heat lightning flashed across the sky, making the clouds look like strange ghost castles on the horizon.

Ruby took the old basket where she kept her beading and needlework. She emptied it out on the ground and handed it to me. "Now, fill this up," she said, "with rocks, your moccasins, anything. *Now*," she ordered.

Wondering what in the world Ruby was up to, I set about

putting in everything we had around us, even some beef jerky, until the basket was completely full.

"Now what?" I asked.

"Now," she said, walking around me still, "that looks like Sin Corazón, when she was most lost." Ruby looked at me questioningly, as if waiting for an answer or a response.

"But I thought you said Sin Corazón was empty and lonely and had a huge hole inside her. That's how I perceived her," I said.

"Well, that's one side of perception. And yes, it's true, she was and is—*was* empty," she said, correcting herself again. "But she was empty because she was so full."

Agnes and Ruby elbowed each other and laughed at my confusion.

"Okay," Ruby said, "now get serious."

We sat down by the basket. I contemplated it for several minutes, tried to imagine Sin Corazón—or myself for that matter—filled with rocks and things.

"You are not filled with the physicalness of your earth walk," Ruby stated. "When you are like Sin Corazón, you are filled with ideas, rigidity, envy, grief, and a stupefied mind that thinks it knows all there is to know. The basket represents that kind of fullness. It's one reason people gather the insignificant waste products of the psychic world into themselves to fill themselves, so they no longer have to confront who they are. Do you see, Little Wolf?"

Letting her words penetrate, I thought of this basket inside me, all filled to the brim. I felt on the edge of nausea with the thought of it. Then finally I realized what she was getting at.

"What you're saying, Ruby, is that when you are full, there is no place for something new."

"Right," Agnes and Ruby said in unison.

By now Agnes had moved and was looking off to the west at the changing world of light on the horizon.

"I see," I said again. "There is no room for creativity. If you're filled with concepts, when you think that what you know is true and important, then creativity simply avoids you."

I laughed. So many times, in my life as an author, I've had to settle myself down into what I realize now was emptiness. Never before had I put words to that feeling. Taking a deep breath and closing my eyes, I dumped out the basket and held it, empty, to my solar plexus for a long time. I let thoughts come toward me, move through my mind, and go out the other side. I didn't hang on to them or grab onto them. Soon my thoughts settled, and life seemed easier. The moment seemed peaceful, and I knew that there was a moment of creativity stalking me, like a story or a dream waiting for me to give it birth and a voice for others to hear.

As I became more silent, the emptiness became more profound. I felt as if the void within me was becoming immense, as if the walls of my womb were pushing out against the armature and the skin of my body. As if my body were dissolving for a moment and I was ceasing to exist in the physical form.

From behind me, Agnes placed her hand on a certain place on my back. She rapped what felt like her knuckles against my spine, and an exquisite state of bliss surrounded me. The universe was filled with many colors and sparkling lights similar to what I find in the sacred dreamtime. I didn't wish to go anywhere in my dreambody; I wished only to stay in this emptiness. But as I did so, I began to realize the depth and the meaning of simplicity, of the extraordinary fragrance of the Great Spirit, of the wisdom it brings into your realization.

Very gently and quietly, Agnes said, "When you are gone, when you are no more, when you have moved into the beat of the mother drum"—on her drum she began to play a very slow heartbeat—"move your consciousness into the beat of the drum and hear yourself. Hear the Great Spirit speaking to you with wisdom.

"When you are out of the way, all possibilities are upon you. Teach your apprentices how to remove their conscious mind from their reckoning. Let them bridge directly into what you call the subconscious, into the dream lodges of the universe. Then you are pure creativity, and nothing then is impossible for you. You are capable of writing the greatest novel, able to conjure the most healing ceremony to present to your people. Beauty surrounds you. Light becomes your servant as you become the servant of light. In the depth of this creativity, you will know your death one day. All that is born upon the good Mother Earth must pass away from our seeing. At those moments we are filled with grief and do not understand, but from your deepest emptiness, there is no separation from all that has ever lived or all that will ever be. For you there are the constant and forever changing trails, always the beginning circling around to be eaten by the endings. You will walk these many trails. They will be like threads on a harp, like energy lines vibrating with music, and you will hold these threads. You will do with them as you will.

"Each of us makes a different design, a different weaving, that we call the soul. When you are filled with this bliss, you are meeting your soul and are becoming acquainted. As this happens, as the first clay pot revealed, you will be changing the cellular structure of what you call your karmic history. For us, your lodges will be filled with others as you move on to build new and sturdier lodges. You are the one, my daughter."

As Agnes finished speaking, what I thought was a meteor crossed the sky from west to east. Emblazoned in blue lavender light, it slowly fell toward the earth and, circling, disappeared before reaching the horizon.

"Perhaps those are our sisters from the faraway," Agnes said. "Perhaps we will talk with them before too long."

19
The Gift of Completion

Agnes and I sat beneath a purple-and-orange sky. She reached out to me, touching my shoulder.

"My daughter, how did the story of Julio and Sin Corazón relate to the teachings of the clay pots? Tell me what you discovered."

I thought for some time with my eyes closed, centering myself and moving into my place of power.

"I realize that in loving someone, I will complete myself within the oneness of all of life. The most extraordinary gift is what only I can give, and it is important to honor how that gift changes someone. In keeping my heart open, I help those I love to enter into situations and experiences they would never have seen or felt on their own.

"That's how the gift of completion is offered. You can intervene in your loving, and fill up someone's holes by extending your energy into them. But if you fool yourself by thinking you've filled yourself and are complete when you aren't, you might be unable to make the transit to wholeness. As soon as you assume that you have it all, energy begins to drain away. But from the moment you are *truly* filled and whole, there's movement and a sense of completion. Then you become filled with radiant light, the breath of God breathing within you.

"In this society we spend a great deal of time blaming those whom we love for our inconsistencies and lapses. It is important and essential that we take responsibility for our own imperfections.

"Sin Corazón and Julio have both changed those aspects of imperfections within themselves so that they can be together.

They are personally filling in the holes for each other, consciously. In a symbolic way Julio Sin Corazón are doing what we are all doing in the actions and crises of our lives; desperately seeking a way of moving out of duality.

"This ancient manuscript talked about how we destroy love by not trusting our vulnerability. Because of the agony of duality so clear in the beginning of their relationship, Julio and Sin Corazón overcame separateness. But if they are not careful, they will search for ways to dominate each other and end the unconditional love that they felt upon their marriage.

"What does this say about the quality of our ability to love? It appears that our culture is only capable of duality. To be whole, you must embrace both of those poles—which is unconditional love. Our parents' love for us may be our only experience of this unconditional love that goes beyond duality. We must begin to love our inner circle unconditionally, in a much bigger way, and develop caring on a very profound level. Where do we learn about this kind of love? Through understanding our relationship to and our awareness of the Great Spirit within us."

Agnes nodded in agreement. Raising her eyebrows in a wide smile, she hugged me. A soft wind had come up from the south, carrying the scent of honeysuckle.

"When do I get to see the next pot?" I asked.

"Soon." Agnes laughed. "When you have earned it as a Twisted Hair."

ENTER A COSMOLOGY OF MYSTERY, MAGIC, AND
POWER WITH LYNN V. ANDREWS . . .

For more than two decades I have been describing my learning and my path. It has been a joy to do this. In continuing my journey, I would be grateful if you would share your insights with me.

You are also invited to join me at my annual spring retreat for four days of ceremony, sacred community, meditation, and healing. In addition, expanded in-depth training is available through the Lynn Andrews Center for Sacred Arts and Training, a home-study course beginning each February. Please call or write for schedule dates and detailed information.

In Spirit,
Lynn V. Andrews

Please send Lynn your name and address so she
can share any new information with you:

Lynn V. Andrews
2934½ Beverly Glen Circle
Box 378
Los Angeles, CA 90077
(800) 726-0082
website: www.lynnandrews.com

About the Author

LYNN V. ANDREWS is a preeminent teacher in the fields of spirituality, personal development, and writing. The author of nineteen books, including the best-selling Medicine Woman series, she is the founder of the Lynn Andrews Center for Sacred Arts and Training, which offers a degree program, online courses, and writers' workshops. For additional information about the author, including her availability for lectures and personal consultations, see www.lynnandrews.com.